# Praise for
# Unleash: The Power to Build the Future You Were Born For

Live with Vision. Lead with Fire.

I have known my good friend Don Brawley for well over two decades. Ever since I met him, he has been not just an encourager but an amplified people-expander, calling leaders to higher heights. His gifts are to give you roots to go deeper and wings to fly higher. In *Unleash: The Power to Build the Future You Were Born For*, you'll find real-life applications of biblical principles. You'll not keep this book to yourself but will share it with family, friends, small groups, and all you love.

**Sam Chand**
Leadership Consultant and Author of *Leadership Pain*

Dr. Don Brawley has created a phenomenal manuscript and blueprint for future leaders to build permanently—not on past failure or temporal successes, but on eternal fundamental principles. *Unleash* empowers readers to shift their mindset, align with the will of God, and move beyond limiting beliefs into a life of faith. This book requires a commitment from each person, regardless of the season you are in, and will guide you to use God's sacred tools to enrich and strengthen your life. I highly recommend *Unleash* to every leader, teacher, and spiritual guide seeking to help people realize their destiny.

**Bishop Tudor Bismark**
Overseer, Jabula New Life Ministries International

Dr. Don Brawley has written with such clarity, passion, and purpose that, page after page, I found myself inspired, challenged, and reminded of what it means to live with vision and lead with fire. What makes *Unleash* so vital is that it is more than theory—it is a blueprint for leaders, pastors, and believers who want to build the future God has designed for them. Dr. Brawley reminds us that the future is not fixed—it is forged—and he shows us how to move from exhaustion to overflow, from drifting to designing, and from fear to faith. This is a life-changing book for pastors, leaders, and every believer who desires to live with vision and lead with fire.

**Bishop Melvin A. Brooks**
Assistant Presiding Bishop, New Jabula New Life Ministries

*Unleash* by Dr. Don Brawley is both timely and Spirit-breathed. It gives leaders, pastors, and believers the framework and language they need to shape the future. What makes this book unique is its rare blend of practical wisdom and biblical depth. This sacred invitation calls us to align with God's design and build a future that blesses families, churches, workplaces, and communities.

**Rev. Dr. Darnell K. Williams, Sr.**
President, North Central University

In *Unleash*, Dr. Don writes with both the biblical depth and practical wisdom that will encourage you to realize it is never too late for any one of us to change, to shift, or to unleash even greater potential inside of us. Leaning on God's wisdom, grace, and providence, Dr. Don guides us through the process of overcoming our uncertainties and crystallizing the preferred future that still exists for you and for me.

**Nicholas Johns**
CEO, LeaderGrow, South Africa

# Unleash

## The Power to Build the Future You were Born For

*Live with Vision. Lead with Fire.*

Don Brawley III

# Unleash

## The Power to Build the Future You were Born For

*Live with Vision. Lead with Fire.*

**Forward by Dale C. Bronner**

© 2025 by Dr. Don Brawley III. All rights reserved.

Published by **Influencers Publishing**
P.O. Box 39820 Snellville, Georgia 30039

Influencers Publishing is privileged to release this work in collaboration with the author. The perspectives and insights within belong solely to the author. Our imprint seal reflects our commitment to exceptional design, meaningful content, and excellence in production.

Some names and identifying details have been changed to protect the privacy of individuals.

No portion of this publication may be copied, stored in a retrieval system, or transmitted in any form or by any means, whether electronic, mechanical, photocopying, recording, or otherwise, without prior written permission from the publisher or author, except as permitted under United States copyright law.

Permission is granted to reproduce brief quotations of up to 500 words for noncommercial use, provided that the following credit line appears:

*Unleash: The Power to Build the Future You Were Born For—Live with Vision. Lead with Fire.* by Dr. Don Brawley III. Used by permission.

All Scripture quotations in this publication are taken from the New International Version (NIV) unless otherwise noted.

Cover by Anointing Productions
Interior design by Pooja Mehra

ISBN: 978-0-9971692-8-7
Library of Congress Control Number
Printed in the United States of America

# Dedications

**Mona,**

From our high school days until today, your love has been the steady flame that ignites my heart. You have believed in me, lifted me when I was weary, and stood beside me in every season. Because of you, I am living into the future I was born for, a future that finds its fullness with you by my side. This book is dedicated to you.

**Impact Church,**

I am honored to call you family, humbled to serve as your pastor, and grateful to walk this journey of life and faith alongside you. Your unwavering commitment to our vision inspires me daily and reminds me that together we are building the future God has called us to fulfill.

# Table of Contents

Foreword .................................................................................. xi

Introduction: When the Future You Imagine No
    Longer Fits What You Were Born For ...................... xiii

## SECTION I: THE FIRE AND THE FRAMEWORK ................ 1

Chapter 1: Four Futures — Discerning the One You
    Were Born For ............................................................. 3

Chapter 2: The Blueprint — Building God's Future
    in Your Life ................................................................ 17

Chapter 3: The Fire Your Future Depends On .............................. 28

## SECTION II: THE PAST AND THE POWER ...................... 41

Chapter 4: Unleashed Power — The Quiet Yes
    That Sparks Revival ................................................... 43

Chapter 5: Break Free for a New Future ....................................... 58

## SECTION III: LIVE WITH VISION. LEAD WITH FIRE ...... 73

Chapter 6: Unleash the Leader Within ......................................... 75

Chapter 7: Living Unleashed — Committing to Your Future ......... 89

Conclusion: Living Unleashed — Your Future Is a Decision Away .................................................................. 102
A Final Prayer .......................................................................... 105
Appendix A: Four Futures Discernment Tool ............................ 107
Appendix B: Four Futures Discernment Tool for Church Leadership Teams ......................................... 109
Appendix C: The 1% Rule for Your Preferred Future .................... 111
Appendix D: The 1% Rule for Team's Preferred Future ................ 112
Appendix E: Chapter Reflection Questions ................................... 114
Endnotes .................................................................................. 117
Meet Dr. Don Brawley III ......................................................... 120
Church and Marketplace Consulting Services ............................. 122
The V.M.O.C. Framework™ ...................................................... 124

# Foreword

**Foreword**
by **Bishop Dale C. Bronner**
Word of Faith Family Worship Cathedral, Austell, Georgia

There are certain books that do not merely inform the mind but ignite the soul. *Unleash: The Power to Build the Future You Were Born For* is one of those books. My dear friend Dr. Don Brawley has given us a timely and timeless gift—a guide that empowers leaders, equips believers, and awakens dreamers to step boldly into the future God has designed for them.

I have known Dr. Brawley for nearly 20 years, and I can testify not only to the depth of his wisdom but to the authenticity of his life. He is not writing from theory, but from testimony. He has walked through the valleys of ministry fatigue, shouldered the weight of leadership, and yet emerged with a fire that still burns brightly for God's people. His words in this book are not simply principles on paper; they are truths proven in the crucible of life and leadership.

This book is not about waiting for the future to reveal itself. It is about discerning God's preferred future and then co-laboring with Him to build it. In a world where so many are drifting, Don's message is clear: you were called to build a future that matters. He challenges us to release fear, embrace courage, and lead with fire.

What strikes me most is how *Unleash* connects the spiritual with the practical. You will find in these pages both the prophetic call to live aligned with heaven's vision and the practical steps to walk it out in your daily decisions. Dr. Brawley shows us that transformation does not always come with thunderclaps and lightning. More often, it begins in the quiet whispers of obedience, in the unseen moments of faithfulness, in the small shifts that create seismic change over time.

As you turn these pages, I encourage you to read not only with your eyes but with your spirit. Allow the words to stir you, challenge you, and ultimately commission you. Because what you hold in your hands is more than a book—it is an invitation to build, to lead, and to live unleashed.

My prayer is that you will receive this work with the same fire in which it was written. And as you do, may you discover that your best days are not behind you; they are ahead, waiting to be built in partnership with the God who called you, equipped you, and destined you for impact.

**Prepare yourself. A future worth building awaits.**

Bishop Dale C. Bronner
Word of Faith Family Worship Cathedral
Austell, Georgia

# INTRODUCTION:

# When the Future You Imagine No Longer Fits What You Were Born For

*"I am confident of this, that He who began a good work in you will carry it on to completion until the day of Christ Jesus."*
—Philippians 1:6 (NIV)

*"The future belongs to those who see possibilities before they become obvious."*[1]
—John Sculley

## The Breaking Point

Over the years, I've met with countless leaders, many of whom appeared successful on the surface, but they were lost and struggling inside.

I know their pain because I've lived it myself.

In 1997, three years after my wife and I left New York to plant our church in Atlanta, I hit a wall. I was working hard as an educator, commuting over an hour each way, while raising two young children who needed my full attention and not just my physical presence.

Our fledgling congregation came with its own constant emergencies: members suddenly leaving the church in throes, couples in crisis, unexpected financial needs, even a family on the verge of homelessness. On top of that, we lost access to our worship space with little notice.

I wore every hat: pastor, counselor, musician, administrator, even janitor. One moment I was playing for worship, the next setting up chairs, counseling couples, or answering late-night calls.

To many, I was their closest confidant. It may have resembled a healthy connection, but in truth, all it meant was that people weren't connecting with one another. Some were even subtly competing for closeness with me. The weight of it all wasn't just heavy; it was quickly becoming unsustainable.

What I came to realize was this—I had imagined a future of thriving ministry, impact, and transformation, but the future I was living no longer fit the one I was born for. The gap between what I imagined and what I experienced nearly undid me.

## Unheard Cries for Help

I tried my best to communicate my struggle. For over six months, I told my leaders, "I am *not* doing well." The responses, though well-meaning, were painfully insufficient: "Just trust God," and "You have faith…you'll be fine." But I wasn't fine. I was unraveling.

Then, one late Saturday night in early October 1997, the dam broke. I turned to my wife and said, "We should just tell the congregation we're done. We'll help each member find another ministry where they can grow, but we can't keep doing this."

I wasn't surprised when the words left my mouth. I had felt it coming for months. What I didn't expect, though, was her response: "I agree. I feel the same way." That stunned me. We had always taken turns being strong for each other. When I was discouraged, she'd ground me in faith and perspective, and vice versa. But this time, we were both empty.

## The Sunday I Quit

That next morning, the first Sunday of the month, we stood before our congregation and announced our resignation. The dream we had left our hometown, family, and jobs for, we were letting it go.

But then something unexpected happened.

Our keyboardist, who wasn't even a member yet, walked up and said, "We won't accept your resignation." He prayed for us. Then one by one, our leaders followed. They finally saw what they had missed—that we were exhausted, not just physically but spiritually. They laid hands on us, prayed, and some even wept, apologizing for not seeing or hearing us sooner.

I can't begin to tell you how much that moment changed my life. It was a turning point, not just for our ministry but for me personally, as a pastor, a husband, and a father.

## The Turning Point

That was the beginning of a liberating mindset shift. I went from believing that if something had to be done, I had to be the one to do it, to embracing a new paradigm—trusting others to shoulder the burden. I realized leadership isn't about independence; it's about *interdependence*.

I began empowering our leaders in ways I hadn't before, trusting them with real responsibility and opportunities to grow. Slowly but surely, they stepped up and began to own the ministry, and I began to reclaim balance. I set boundaries. I protected time with my family. I started leading from overflow, not from exhaustion.

## The Call Confirmed

But now, three decades after that weary Sunday morning in October, I can say with clarity: Nothing has been more fulfilling, more deeply rewarding, or more tailor-made for me than pastoring Impact Church, which I continue to lead to this day.

Were there challenges? Absolutely. Were there frustrations, setbacks, and delays? Without question.

But it was out of that breaking point and walking through the burnout, the honesty, and the rebuilding that something unexpected was born in me: a passion to help other pastors avoid what I went through—a calling to equip leaders to carry the weight of ministry in healthy, sustainable ways. To build churches that don't just grow in numbers, but flourish in vitality, health, and longevity.

Perhaps you see yourself in my story.

Maybe you know what it's like to wake up in the middle of the night and think, "How did I get here?"

Maybe you feel stuck in the inertia of decisions you don't remember making. You wonder if it's too late to change, to shift, or to unleash something greater inside of you.

## The Future Isn't Fixed—It's Forged

Here's the liberating truth—The future isn't fixed, it's forged. It's not sealed by your past or secured by your present. It's not a script carved in stone, but a canvas shaped by every choice, every breath, every act of faith.

Winston Churchill said, "Success is not final, failure is not fatal: It is the courage to continue that counts."[2] Whether you stand in triumph or tread through disappointment, neither defines you. Your story is still unfolding. It isn't dictated by what has been but by what you decide to do next.

Your story is not a sentence; it's a scroll still being written.

You may be standing on the mountaintop, successful but still restless. Or staring at a closed door, wondering if you've waited too long or wasted too much time. Wherever you are, you're shaping what's to come, moment by moment, decision by decision.

Most never realize how much power God has placed within them. They assume life happens to them, not through them. They confuse momentum with calling and mistake indecision for divine timing.

> **Every future is being built now.**

But hear this—Every future is being built now. Whether wasted, welcomed, or wild, each one rises the same way: one decision at a time.

So, the question is not if you're building a future, but what kind of future are you building? Because all futures aren't equal, some are accidental, some intentional, and only one is aligned with the life God designed you to live. And the way you reach that future isn't through one dramatic moment but through steady, unseen choices.

> **Transformation is not a single event—it's a thousand small shifts in the same direction.**

Transformation rarely comes like lightning. It begins in the quiet, in the choices no one sees. Breakthroughs don't shout—they whisper.

That's why this book isn't about waiting for a breakthrough. It's about becoming the kind of person who builds one.

It's about stepping into the power God has already placed within you: the power to choose differently, to align intentionally, and to shape a future that doesn't just happen to you but happens *through* you.

So, if you've ever felt stuck...
If you've sensed a stirring deep inside that there's more...
If you've glimpsed a future that feels bigger than your past, but weren't sure how to step toward it...

Then I have just one question: Are you ready to build the future you were born for? Because the next decision you make may not only change your direction; it can change everything. But before you build forward, you'll have to be honest about what you're carrying now.

## The Weight You're Carrying (And the Future It's Creating)

You've done everything you were told would lead to purpose: You've worked hard, followed the plan, and checked all the boxes. And yet, there's a quiet ache that won't leave you alone. A still, persistent whisper echoing in the corners of your soul: "This isn't it. There has to be more." You're right. You *were* made for more; but instead of running toward that "more," you find yourself...stuck.

Maybe you're a leader who's lost your fire. There was a time when work felt like worship and every task overflowed from a sense of divine purpose. But now? You're showing up out of duty instead of devotion. You're managing obligations instead of moving hearts. The joy has faded, and your fire's all but burned out.

Unfortunately, life doesn't offer time-outs. Even when you feel stuck, it doesn't pause while you find your footing. Every day you delay, every decision you avoid, every moment you spend second-guessing becomes another seed sown into a future you never intended to build.

## Standing at the Crossroads

Deep down, you know it. Opportunities keep slipping through your fingers. You're drained from giving without being filled. And you ache at the thought of being in the same place five years from now, with less time and fewer chances to change it. That's the real pain: not just where you are, but the fear of staying there forever.

This is the crossroads: You can keep hoping things will change, you can keep telling yourself that someday, somehow, it will all work out, or you can decide right now to shift the trajectory of your life and leadership.

No matter how paralyzed you feel, you are not powerless. No matter how long you've been waiting, God has not forgotten you. He hasn't changed His mind about you or your calling.

The future is being built today, and if you don't choose to shape it with faith and intention, someone or something else will. So, the question is not whether you have power. The question is: Will you unleash it? Will you build it? When you do, everything else starts to shift.

## The Future You're Meant to Build

Now, imagine waking up with clarity. No longer going through the motions, you rise with purpose, knowing exactly where you're headed and why. The weight of uncertainty lifts, replaced by the steady peace of alignment. The decisions that once felt heavy now feel holy because you finally understand how each one shapes the future you were born to build.

Imagine yourself stepping into leadership, motherhood, or ministry not from a place of exhaustion or duty, but from overflow. No longer drained by constant demands, you now lead with confidence. Your presence, your influence, and your words all carry weight. And this time, you can see it, you can feel it: Your life is making impact in real time.

Picture standing in front of that opportunity that once terrified you, and instead of shrinking back, you say: "Yes. I'm ready."

No more second-guessing.
No more waiting for permission.
No more paralysis by what-ifs and not-yets.

The fear that once held you back? Powerless. The self-doubt that whispered you're not enough? Dismantled and replaced by the truth: I am equipped for this. The uncertainty that made you hesitate? Now replaced by momentum.

## Your Courage Becomes A Catalyst

And perhaps most powerful of all: imagine how your life begins to ripple. Your courage becomes a catalyst. Your shift ignites shifts in others. Your decision to rise gives someone else permission to do the same.

You start to see breakthroughs, not just in your life, but in your family, your team, your ministry, your community. When you step into the future God designed for you, you become a door through which others walk into their own.

And one day, as you look back, weeks, months, years from now, you won't see a life that merely "happened". You'll see a life you co-built with God. A future formed by design and not by default.

And the best part? That future isn't far off. It's not unreachable. It's not reserved for someone else. It's yours! The only question now is: Will you step into it?

## Unleash: The Power to Build the Future You Were Born For

This isn't another book filled with church cliches, generic motivational phrases, or abstract theories. Unleash is about igniting God's fire within you and equipping you with practical tools to shift your mindset, reshape your future, and unlock the full potential of your life and leadership.

It's your invitation to discern and step into the future He's set before you, and to join Him in building it. You don't have to settle for a future that seems inevitable based on where you've been. You influence your trajectory. And when you align yourself with God's wisdom, embrace a renewed mindset, and take intentional action, you can unleash the life you were meant to live.

Are you ready to stop passively watching life happen and start stepping into the future God has for you? Are you willing to challenge your old ways of thinking, release the fears that have held you captive, and step into the power you have in shaping what comes next? Are you ready to live with vision, lead with fire, and burn with purpose so that your life sets others ablaze?

If the answer is "yes" and you're ready to stop drifting and start building, turn the page. Your future is waiting.

# SECTION I

# The Fire and the Framework

(Chapters 1-3)

## CHAPTER 1

# Four Futures – Discerning the One You Were Born For

*"For I know the plans I have for you," declares the Lord, "plans to prosper you and not to harm you, plans to give you hope and a future.*
— Jeremiah 29:11 (NIV)

*"Watch to see where God is working and join Him in His work."*[1]
— Henry Blackaby

### Where Have You Come From…And Where Are You Going?

In an early episode of the Bible, we find Hagar lost in the desert wilderness. After being taken from her homeland and suffering abuse and oppression, she finally crumbles under the weight of a life rapidly spinning out of her control. Pregnant with her master's child, she flees into the desert wasteland, hundreds of miles from her homeland, with nowhere to go.

It is in this wilderness that she encounters the Angel of the Lord. Mercifully, He does not chastise her or shame her, but instead, nudges her with a gentle question:

"Where have you come from, and where are you going?" (Genesis 16:8)

Hagar could only answer the first half of the question. She knew where she had come from: a place of pain, rejection, and abandonment. What she could not yet see was where she was going. And in many ways, that's where we may find ourselves: fluent in our history, yet clueless about our destiny.

As you step into the Four Futures, do not read only with your mind. Listen with your spirit. Let each one reveal not only what could be, but what must be if you are willing to choose it. While all Four Futures offer insight, this book focuses especially on two: the probable future, which is the path you are on if nothing changes, and the preferred future, which is the one God designed for you to walk in. The greatest transformation happens when you move from what is likely to what is divinely designed.

God still whispers the same question today. It's not meant to shame us but to *shift* our thinking.

## A Whisper in the Wilderness

Perhaps this book is His wilderness whisper to you, a divine interruption not to expose your failures, but to awaken your future. Maybe, this is more than a page; it's a portal, a heaven-sent invitation to name the future you were born to build.

Too often, we miss the future heaven has prepared, not because it's hidden, but because we're too distracted to see it. We look backward, rehearsing old wounds, clutching regrets that no longer serve us. We look downward, overwhelmed by present burdens, tangled in what we lack. We look inward, doubting our worth, questioning if we are enough. And we look outward, comparing our journey to someone else's highlight reel.

But rarely do we look *forward*. We forget to lift our eyes, to still our hearts, and to ask the questions that shape our destiny: *What could be possible? What might God still want to build through me?*

These distractions lead us to miss a vital truth: The outcomes of our lives are not the result of where we intended to go, but where we are *going*.

That's why the enemy loves them.

Why bother destroying your future when he can distract you from it?

But what if you stopped and looked up? What if you dared to see what heaven sees?

## Where Are You Headed?

Your future is not a fixed destination. It is a living landscape, shaped by your decisions, refined by your delays, and orchestrated by the hand of God. That's why parents, pastors, leaders, and all who influence others must see clearly. You are not just building a future for yourself but for your family, your team, your church, and your legacy.

To lead well, you must see clearly. And to see clearly, you must understand the terrain ahead.

Four Futures: Discerning the One You Were Born For

In the field of strategic foresight, leaders are trained to navigate *four types of futures*: the **probable**, the **possible**, the **plausible**, and the **preferred**[2]. Each offers a distinct lens on what could unfold, and grasping these frameworks can mean the difference between drifting aimlessly and stepping boldly into the future heaven intended for you.

There are four primary lenses through which to view your future (see chart in Appendix A):

- **The probable future** – What's *most likely to happen* if nothing changes. Often marked by resignation and quiet frustration, especially when you know deep down you were made for more.
- **The plausible future** – What *realistically might happen*. This future pushes you to participate, but is still constrained by your expectations, safety, and a limited imagination.
- **The possible future** – What *could happen*. This future awakens your imagination to take your gifts and talents in bold new directions. It's the best of what earth has to offer, but falls short of Heaven's complete design.
- **The preferred future** – What *should happen*. This is the future heaven designed for you. It doesn't come easily, but it calls you to rise boldly, with vision, faith, and courage.

Awareness of these futures opens the door to participation in your future. No longer drifting from outcome to outcome, you become a navigator, steering your life into alignment with God's vision.

## From Drift to Design

Your life is a tapestry stretched across the loom of time. Every decision, relationship, encounter, and turn weaves into what will one day be revealed. You cannot control every strand, but you can choose the pattern you pursue.

Will you let chaos dictate the weave, or will you shape it with intention, vision, and grace? The Four Futures framework helps you step back from the loom to see not only what is, but what could be.

> **A great life is not stumbled into. It is crafted with vision, effort, and divine direction.**

Without them, you drift into grayness, your leadership settles, your fire fades, and your future conforms to what is probable or merely plausible. Not because that's all God has for you, but because entropy is easier than effort.

God has not called you to rehearse yesterday. He has called you to shape tomorrow.

## The Sanctuary of Imagination
Each of these futures has implications, not just for your personal life, but for your leadership, your ministry, and the Church itself. Naming and understanding them isn't just a mental exercise; it is a spiritual act, a leadership imperative.

Because nowhere is the tension between comfort and calling more visible than in the future of our congregations. Each future paints a different portrait of the Church: probable drifts, plausible survives, possible imagines, and preferred fulfills God's dream. And it is your mindset that determines which one you will walk into.

## Your Mindset Is Your Map
To step into your preferred future, the one aligned with heaven's design, you need more than ambition. You need a growth mindset shaped by a holy conviction that you can be formed, stretched, and transformed through grace, obedience, and Spirit-empowered effort.

It's not only about dreaming big; it's about thinking differently. What you believe about change shapes how you face challenges. If you believe you're stuck, you'll remain stuck. If you believe you can grow, then you will.

Your future isn't limited by your past; it's limited by the mindset you bring into your next season.

Psychologist Carol Dweck defines a growth mindset as "the belief that your basic qualities can be cultivated"[3]. It embraces challenge, persists through difficulty, and views setbacks not as final but as refining. It is the difference between settling for what is and daring to believe in what could be.

## Standing On the Edge of Possibility

When you believe change is possible, you live and lead as if it is inevitable. But if you decide transformation cannot happen, the possible future dims, and the preferred future slips out of reach.

That's why unleashing your future doesn't begin with strategy; it begins with surrender, surrendering assumptions, limitations, and the false stories that have quietly shaped your expectations. Only then can you dream again, decide differently, and build the future you were born for.

So, let's begin the work of discernment.

## Unpacking the Four Futures

Imagine you stand at a branching road, with four futures and four destinations before you. The first you see is also the most common, the most comfortable, and often the most costly: the probable future.

### 1. The Probable Future — Headed There by Default

The **probable future** is the road most traveled, not because it's best but because it's familiar. It is shaped by your current habits, unconscious momentum, and invisible currents like societal expectations, economic shifts, and cultural pressures. Left unchallenged, these will sweep you toward an outcome you never consciously chose.

Autopilot is the gateway to your probable future. When you stop making intentional decisions and start coasting, repeating routines, avoiding reflection, and settling for comfort, you drift not toward what is meaningful but toward what is merely likely.

Living on autopilot is like setting cruise control in the wrong direction. You keep moving, but drift further from purpose. It feels safe, but it robs you of vision. It trades purpose for patterns and reduces calling to maintenance. If you do not choose your future, your habits will—and they will always choose what is easy, not what is holy.

Think of it this way: skip the gym once, then again, then again. Soon the habit is gone, the weight creeps in, and energy drains away, not because you chose decline but because you stopped choosing growth.

## Gradually then Suddenly

King Saul was chosen by God, anointed as Israel's first king, and his reign began in promise. But over time, a pattern emerged: insecurity, disobedience, and self-preservation. He ignored Samuel's counsel. He chose image over obedience. And though the crown lingered, his calling slowly unraveled…because he stopped choosing it.

Eventually, the prophet spoke what had already taken root in Saul's soul:

> *"Because you have rejected the word of the Lord, He has rejected you as king."*
> (1 Samuel 15:23)

Saul's downfall wasn't sudden; it was a slow erosion that ended in collapse. As my good friend and leadership expert, Dr. Samuel R. Chand, wisely puts it: "It happens gradually, then suddenly."

That's how the probable future works, not with explosions, but with erosion. First, the signs are subtle. Commitment fades. Health is postponed. Relationships crack. And one day, it all collapses, seemingly out of nowhere, though the drift began long before.

This isn't just personal; it's organizational, too. The same drift that derails individuals can quietly dismantle churches. What's true for your heart is true for your house of worship.

But hear this: *probable* is not *permanent*. One surrendered decision can reroute everything. One spark can reignite what's gone cold and shift the trajectory of your life, your leadership, and your legacy. The ink isn't dry. Heaven's Author still holds the pen and invites you to pick up yours again.

While the probable future shows what's likely if nothing changes, the plausible future opens your eyes to what might unfold if current patterns shift, even slightly.

## 2. The Plausible Future — Safe but Small

On the surface, the **plausible future** shows signs of life. Congregations slowly rebuild. Digital rhythms are learned. Programs relaunch. Sanctuaries refill. Volunteers return. But too often, vision shrinks to fit survival.

We aim low, hit the target, and call it success, mistaking stability for transformation. Churches begin to celebrate maintenance as their mission, not because they have fulfilled their calling, but because they have adjusted their expectations.

It is like a couple stuck in survival mode. They talk, eat dinner at the same table, and do just enough to keep the home together. On the surface, things look stable. But instead of pursuing deeper healing and renewed love, they settle for coexistence. The relationship doesn't die, but it doesn't thrive either.

This is what happens when the memory of hardship becomes the boundary of imagination, when returning to what was feels safer than reaching for what could be.

In Scripture, it is Israel at Kadesh-Barnea, camped at the very edge of promise. God had spoken. The land was before them. But fear drowned out their faith. They did not go back, but they did not go forward either. Not because God said no, but because they stopped dreaming.

## When Vision Shrinks to Fit Survival

Kadesh-Barnea wasn't a failure of movement; it was a failure of imagination. The God who delivered them was ready to empower them, but they chose safety over surrender and familiarity over faith.

That's the plausible future: faithful in form but hesitant in spirit. Rebuilding, yet not risking. Singing old songs, afraid to write new ones. It looks like faithfulness, but it's fear disguised as tradition.

When fear grows louder than faith, hesitation becomes championed as wisdom. The plausible future leaves us near the edge of transformation but never crossing over. We cling to the wilderness "just in case," celebrating the past while avoiding the fight for the future. What it saves in risk, it loses in destiny.

But God does not meet us at the altar of ease. He meets us in the stretch, where trust dares to outweigh uncertainty. The possible future dares us to imagine what could happen if we surrendered limitation and let faith lead the way.

### 3. The Possible Future — One Bold Move Away

The **possible future** is a wide-open field. It is what could unfold, for better or worse, if you dare to look past your limitations. It is the door that opens when others slam shut. It shows up in surprise promotions, divine detours, and miracles hidden in ordinary moments. It whispers, *your story isn't over.*

Remember Nineveh where Jonah declared judgment, but repentance rewrote the ending. What seemed inevitable became avoidable. That's the power of choosing possibility when probability looms large.

Sometimes, possibility comes cloaked in disruption. When the pandemic hit, churches rooted in prayer didn't collapse; they adapted. Resilience isn't seized in crisis; it's forged in culture, sacrifice, and hidden faithfulness. And sometimes that possibility looks as simple as launching family devotions, mentoring a couple in crisis, or starting the ministry that once stirred your soul. Small seeds can grow into transformation.

And I've seen that same truth in my own journey. When God called us to leave New York and plant a church in Atlanta, possibility showed up in ways that almost pulled us off course. That's the danger of possibility; it can be a gift, but if you're not careful, it can also distract you from God's preferred future.

## My Story of Possibility

When God called us to leave New York and plant a church in Atlanta, possibilities began flooding in. A new job opportunity opened near home. Well-meaning friends reminded us we could easily plant a church on Long Island where family, friends, and followers were ready to support us. The possible future would have been easier, safer, and it even seemed more promising; but I'm certain it would have proven unfulfilling and, in the end, far more costly. We chose obedience over opportunity.

This is your story too. A podcast, a prayer, or a passing word could launch your next chapter. One small yes can open a door you never imagined, and one ordinary moment can become the birthplace of your breakthrough. God may still want to raise what you've resigned to routine.

Looking back, I see the distinction between the *possible* and *preferred* futures clearly. Often, the price of admission to God's preferred future is laying down the possible one you had in mind. I've learned that possibility can open many doors, but only obedience leads you through the one God designed, and that is where the preferred future begins. It's not just what *could* happen; it's what *should* happen.

### 4. The Preferred Future — Built by Design, Not by Drift

The preferred future is the one you were born for. The one aligned with His vision, shaped by your obedience, and fueled by purpose. A future not imagined out of fear or ambition but spiritually discerned through faith.

In my consulting work, I've walked with pastors and teams who aren't just dreaming of what could be; they are building it, sketching revival, and constructing ministries that reflect heaven's heartbeat. Spirit-led and purpose-driven, they carry vision for the future God intends.

It's like someone whom God stirs to pursue a degree later in life. They study when they're weary, press on when others quit, and sacrifice comfort for calling.

Make no mistake; the cost of the preferred is the willingness to sacrifice the *possible*. Comfort, convenience, and easier options will always compete for your yes. But only obedience secures the future God designed.

## A Church's Preferred Future

I think of two dying churches I served in Flint, Michigan—one Black, one White. One was young and vibrant but lacked resources. The other had resources but was aging and declining. On paper, both futures looked bleak but together they discerned something more than possible; they reflected the unity of Heaven on Earth. They touched the preferred. They laid down pride, merged, and built a new house of worship that now thrives. Not chance, not drift, but obedience.

This future is never stumbled into. It is seized through Spirit-filled intention and Spirit-led resolve. It is summoned by faith, forged in sweat, and secured by obedience. Nehemiah embodied this well.

## When Heaven's Blueprint Meets Earthly Obedience

When Nehemiah heard Jerusalem's walls lay in ruins, he didn't just grieve; he mobilized. He fasted and prayed. He cast vision to a weary people. Where others saw rubble, he saw renewal. And in just 52 days, what once lay in waste became a city reborn; not by might, but by divine resolve.

Visionary leadership doesn't wait for the right moment; it creates it. It runs into the rubble and builds anyway. That is how preferred futures are born.

Then same principle applies at home: when a mother prays, when a father leads devotion, when a couple seeks counsel before crisis. These are not small acts. They are kingdom seeds, planted in obedience, watered by grace, and destined to bear fruit.

Whether in the pulpit, boardroom, or living room, the principle remains: preferred futures don't emerge from activity alone. They are forged in the culture you cultivate, the leaders you disciple, and the systems you align with heaven's design.

## The Cost and Call of the Preferred Future

While the possible future stirs hope, the preferred future requires surrender. It is not about what could happen, but about aligning with what God has ordained.

Abraham longed for a son, but God envisioned a nation. He nearly settled for the possible when God had destined him for the preferred. In the end, it was not his dream that qualified him, but his willingness to lay that dream on the altar. Sacrifice was the doorway into God's promise, and it remains the doorway for us today.

> ...the possible future, the one we *could* build, often becomes the enemy of the preferred future, the one we *should* build

In the same way, we often choose familiar routines over faith-stretching risks. We stay in broken systems, unfulfilling careers, and toxic relationships because we fear the cost of change. Make no mistake: the Possible Future, the one we could build, often becomes the enemy of the Preferred Future, the one we should build, when comfort becomes our compass.

Here's the distinction: goals can lead to the possible, but only God leads to the preferred.

### The Road Heaven Built for You

Be warned: the preferred future is not the easier road. It often demands more tears, more prayer, and more risk. But it's the road Jesus took, the road Paul ran, the road Nehemiah walked. And it's the road God is inviting you to travel.

In the ***Unleash* Masterclass,** I walk you through how to identify that future with clarity and courage, helping you recognize heaven's vision over your life and how to co-build it with God.

Maybe it's a reconciled family, a debt-free household, or a mentoring movement that outlives you. Maybe it's a marketplace ministry transforming your industry. Maybe it's raising up Spirit-empowered disciples.

Whatever it is, it's already designed in Heaven, and the Architect is with you.

Now that you've seen the terrain of the Four Futures, you can discern where your feet have been walking and where your heart longs to go. But naming your future is only the beginning. The question remains: how will you get there?

If Chapter 1 was a compass, what comes next is a blueprint. The future God calls you into does not appear by accident; it is built in alignment with Heaven's design. And it begins with the bricks you lay today.

Let's take the next step together. **Want the full Four Futures Discernment Tool + leadership team version?** Download the full Unleash Toolkit free at www.donbrawley.com/unleash or scan the QR code below.

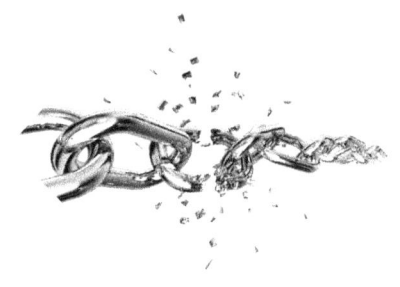

CHAPTER 2

# The Blueprint—Building God's Future in Your Life

*Unless the Lord builds the house, the builders labor in vain.*
— Psalm 127:1 (NIV)

*"The best way to predict the future is to create it."*[1]
— Peter Drucker

## Building What Lasts

The Great Wall of China stands today as one of the most awe-inspiring feats of human perseverance and engineering, but it wasn't built in a day, a year, or even a lifetime. It was constructed, brick by brick, over centuries by ordinary people doing ordinary work with extraordinary consistency. What began as a scattered effort eventually became a fortified monument that can now be seen from space. In the same way, your future won't simply appear; it must be assembled, shaped, and stewarded over time. **It must be constructed.**

As leaders, we often overestimate what we can do in a day and underestimate what we can build in a year. We chase sudden breakthroughs instead of trusting in the slow momentum of daily obedience. However, God's greatest works are rarely microwaved; they are marinated and formed over time. His boldest visions rise from the hidden bricks we faithfully lay when no one is watching.

In this chapter, we will discover the power of daily rhythms and habits to change the course of our lives and build a masterpiece structure. We'll see how even minor shifts in these habits can awaken us from the drift of probable living and construct the future we were born for.

## Building Wisely

If you were handed one brick a day and told to build a wall that would one day protect your family, your ministry, and your future, how carefully would you place it? Would you toss it without thought, hoping it lands in the right spot? Or would you pause, pray, and position it with intention, knowing that what you're building today could shelter generations tomorrow?

The reality is, you're already doing this. With every thought you dwell on, every decision you make, and every action you take, you are laying bricks into the future. Every time you choose discipline over distraction, you lay a brick. Every time you speak life instead of criticism, you place a brick. Every time you pursue peace, walk in integrity, or obey the Spirit's nudge, another brick is set in place.

But the same is also true for the reverse. What if, instead of patience, you choose a hasty reaction, or instead of faithfulness, a compromised conviction? Fear-driven choices and flesh-driven decisions are also building a future. Laid without care, they'll create fractures in the very structure you were depending on to carry your future.

That's why Scripture reminds us, "By wisdom a house is built, and through understanding it is established; through knowledge its rooms are filled with rare and beautiful treasures" (Proverbs 24:3–4 NIV).

Wisdom, understanding, and knowledge…notice that these aren't qualities attained in a moment, but the products of daily discipline.

Our use of them, and the lack thereof, will one day determine if our structure stands the test of time or crumbles under pressure.

Noah exemplified this well. Despite never seeing a droplet of rain, he wisely trusted in the Lord and followed his guidance. He built the ark faithfully, day by day and plank by plank, until obedience became rhythm, trusting that God would honor his discipline and preserve his family for generations to come.

Building won't always look miraculous. In fact, it often looks mundane. But the same kind of quiet, steady obedience that Noah lived by is the same kind God honors in you.

## The 1% Rule: When Small Becomes Significant

It can be easy to think of our lives as the culmination of several capstone moments: finishing school, landing a first job, starting a business, or getting married. These moments, whether celebrated or regretted, stand out in bold print across the story of our lives. Yet the truth is, none of them appeared in isolation. Each was shaped by a thousand smaller decisions—habits, words, and actions that built the foundation for the moment we now remember. It is these small, and often forgotten, decisions that quietly shaped the outcome.

This highlights an essential truth—you don't build your future in the future; you build it now. The question is: Are you building it on purpose?

Building doesn't have to be dramatic to be effective. In fact, the best way to intentionally build your future is *incrementally*. By utilizing the 1% Rule, you can leverage small, daily shifts that build a major impact over time[2]. Done consistently, these 1% growth spurts will steadily mold you out of probable living and into the person God created you to be.

Opportunities for 1% improvement are all around us: the mother who prays for her child before school, the pastor discipling a young leader over coffee, and the father who chooses gentleness in a moment of anger. Though small in the moment, when stacked on yesterday's obedience, today's surrender, and tomorrow's trust, these small steps become a fortified wall, strong enough to carry a legacy of faithfulness for generations to come.

What would it look like for you to be one percent more courageous, patient, or obedient? This is how simple habits become baptized with the supernatural and disciplines become your destiny. God doesn't demand perfection; He honors persistence. He doesn't require leaps; He blesses steps. And He measures greatness not by what others see, but by the unseen choices you make when no one's watching.

So, ask yourself:

- What's one small shift I can make today?
- What's the one brick I've been ignoring?
- What's one area where I need to stop waiting for a breakthrough and start laying bricks?

Because when you give God your 1%, He breathes on it, and what feels small becomes significant. And that's how revival begins, not in the spotlight, but in the rhythm of surrender.

## An Ancient Rhythm

Scripture often speaks to us in verbs: *walk, seek, dwell*…These are not occasional acts but holy rhythms—meditative, intentional movements that mold our spirit and set our feet on course for Heaven's preferred future. They form us day by day, layer by layer, and choice by choice.

The book of Acts shows us how these daily rhythms affected the Early Church. Acts 2 tells us that, "Every day they continued…"

*Every day*. Not only on Sundays. Not only when they were in the spotlight or celebrated. It signifies that they persisted, whether they "felt it" or noticed a change. They committed themselves daily, joyfully, and faithfully. They regularly sold their possessions to aid others in need, shared meals in fellowship, prayed together, and supported one another.

And what is the result? Verse 47 says, "And the Lord added to their number daily those who were being saved."

Seeing a pattern?

God breathed on their ordinary. It didn't have to be flashy, and though it sometimes moved fast, it was built through faithfulness. Through daily devotion, humble routine, and steady repetition, the Spirit moved. Through their faithfulness, the Kingdom advanced, and the Church was born. And like we saw with the Great Wall, we once again see ordinary people, doing ordinary things to build an extraordinary Church; only this time, God is building a monument that will stand for all eternity.

And what you live daily becomes what you leave behind. There is revival in your rhythm. There is glory in your grind. There is power in your pattern, when it's aligned with heaven.

> **Because what you do daily becomes who you are**

So don't underestimate the ordinary. God still anoints the faithful. He still breathes on the steady. And the future is still being formed, one quiet yes at a time.

But here's the tension: building without clarity can be just as dangerous as not building at all.

## Driven but Drifting

The probable future happens by default. The preferred future is built through small, strategic choices. But even the best builders fail without the blueprint to guide them, as I once did.

Early in my pastorate, I was driven by urgency but unclear on direction. I was preaching weekly, launching programs, and saying yes to every opportunity that came my way. From the outside, it looked like momentum. But behind the scenes? I was exhausted.

The external pressure of trying to build without a blueprint led me to confusion and burnout. I hadn't paused to ask God what He was building or clarified what I should be aiming for. Soon, the cracks began to show in my strained relationships, blurred priorities, and eventual vision drift.

One morning in prayer, I sensed God whisper,

*"You're working hard, but you won't last. You can keep building, but not like this."*

Essentially, He was saying: *"You have activity but no alignment."* I knew that if I wanted to build something worthwhile, I'd have to surrender my dreams and expectations of what that would look like. That moment broke me, but it also began to rebuild me.

That season changed everything for me. Once I entered a posture of surrender, a new clarity emerged. It changed the trajectory of my leadership and taught me that speed without direction is the fastest way to burnout.

When you feel a drive but no sense of direction, it's an indicator that you need to consult with the Architect. You may be building without a blueprint.

## Building Without A Blueprint

In 2004, my wife and I took on the challenge of building a house from the ground up.

We had three children between the ages of four and eleven, as well as my mother, who was ill, living with us. With all of us under one roof, it made sense for us to design a new build that could comfortably fit us all.

Looking back at the countless decisions, each tiny detail, I can't imagine building that house without a blueprint. Without it, our investment of time, money, and energy would have collapsed into disappointment: walls leaning, doors hanging crooked, and the foundation ready to give way.

No one in their right mind would dare to build a house without a plan, yet we'll often build our lives without one and hardly think twice about it.

Yes, even with a plan, storms will come. A blueprint is never a promise of calm seas, but it does anchor us, giving us the framework to build our future on solid ground. And when the storms come, and they will, we can be confident that though the walls may bend, they will not break.

So, let me ask you: What kind of builder are you? Because the future isn't just ahead of you; it's rising beneath your feet. And today, you hold the trowel.

## Default Builders vs. Intentional Builders

Some live like accidental builders: drifting, reacting, and laying bricks with no blueprint.

Intentional builders are different. They rise with fire in their eyes and blueprints in their hearts. They don't just "hope things work out"; they build toward a vision with conviction. Each brick laid, every habit practiced, every sacrifice made aligns with a future shaped in prayer.

They are not victims of circumstance. They are sacred apprentices of the Master Architect. Storms may rage, yet they keep building, anchored in faith and steady in purpose. This kind of builder isn't always seen, but they are always significant.

Think of the small-town pastor with no spotlight, no stage, only people, a pulpit, and a calling. He does not measure success by the world's standards, but by lives touched through his ministry. Week after week, he preaches. He prays. He visits. He clings to the vision God has given him. One more life saved. One more life changed.

That's him building, quietly, faithfully, diligently. His story may seem small, but it carries a greater truth: intentional builders don't crave applause; they carry vision. They don't chase noise; they chase legacy. They rest in the knowledge that quiet integrity shapes the world. And they know this: before it reshapes anyone else's world, it must first shape their own.

## Your Life Is a Construction Site

Nothing captures the weight and power of every decision quite like the story I heard years ago about a seasoned builder named Carl and his longtime employer, Bob.

Carl was nearing retirement. After years of excellence, fatigue had set in, and he was ready to be finished. On what he assumed would be his final project, he began to cut corners: choosing cheap materials, overlooking hidden flaws, rushing the timeline, and doing whatever it took to finish quickly.

Then came the twist: the home he was building was a gift from Bob—for him!

All the shortcuts he had taken were now his to live with. Carl thought what he built didn't matter much, but he had been building his own future all along.

So are you.

Jesus said, "Suppose one of you wants to build a tower. Won't you first sit down and count the cost?" (Luke 14:28).

> **Whatever you build today, you will live in tomorrow**

Intentional builders plan. They count. They persist. They don't build for applause; they build to last.

We are all building something. The only question is how? Are you building by default, passively reacting to what's in front of you? Or are you building by design, with vision, prayer, and the future in mind?

## Are You Building by Default?

Here's how you'll know that you are building by default:

- You react more than you reflect.
- You're repeating patterns without evaluating impact.
- You haven't revisited your vision in months, maybe even years.

These aren't minor signs; they're warning lights on the dashboard of your destiny. Default building feels productive…until it crumbles under pressure. Because busyness is not the same as purpose. And hustle is not the same as Spirit-led living.

Don't confuse motion with mission. A leader can preach to crowds and leave no legacy. A parent can provide without presence. A believer can attend without transformation. But a builder who pours into the few, prays in the quiet, and chooses faith over fame, builds a legacy that remains.

Every small choice, moment of patience, word of grace, and quiet prayer is a brick.

And remember this: you're not building alone. For, as the Psalmist declared:

> *"Unless the Lord builds the house, the builders labor in vain"*
> (Psalm 127:1).

God is not just watching your work; He's working with you.

This isn't a call to step back. It's a call to step in—with God. Even when the work feels slow or unseen, remember you are part of something sacred. You are building a future strong enough to shelter generations.

So, will you cut corners in the dark or build with vision, sacrifice, and trust? Because the future doesn't just depend on your dreams, it depends on your decisions.

And it's being built now, one choice at a time. The moment you build with purpose, resistance rises, because every God-given future must be fought for.

## Obstacles and How to Overcome Them

Anyone who's ever undertaken the challenge of building something knows that every construction will encounter unexpected obstacles.

When we are faced with resistance, it can be easy to think we are going the wrong way. When our progress slows, doubts start to creep in; fatigue and disappointments mount like storms, and the vision we once could see clearly dims.

But remember Moses. His forty years in the wilderness weren't wasted; they were preparation for his calling. They were essential for the greater work that God would do in his coming years, and the character needed to maintain it. The waiting wasn't a detour; it was part of the build.

Obstacles aren't roadblocks; they're tests of faith, endurance, and trust. They sharpen your tools and grow your character. They drive you deeper into God's presence and force you to depend on His direction. So, when the walls tremble, anchor deeper. Adjust, but don't abandon the blueprint. Pray like Nehemiah. Push like Noah. Lead like Moses. And keep laying bricks.

Because every challenge overcome becomes a stronger foundation.

Every time you place a brick in faith, when quitting would be easier, when answers are far, when you choose faith over fear, growth over comfort, and forgiveness over pride, you can be confident that those bricks matter. They are shaping something eternal.

## Building Begins Now

So build anyway. And know that every choice is a seed. Leader, laborer, pastor what you plant today will shape someone else's tomorrow.

Like Noah, every obedient act becomes a beam, part of a vessel built not just for survival, but for legacy. It may feel small now, but no pause, prayer, or quiet yes goes unnoticed by heaven.

That's why I wrote this book: to help you discern, decide, and build with bold faith until what God promised becomes what you walk in.

And it all begins now.

Let this be your brick, the one where you stop drifting and start building. The one where you silence the noise and listen for God's design again. The one where delay becomes determination, fear becomes faith, and routine becomes rhythm.

You are not behind, and you are not building alone. The Master Architect is with you. Take the brick and lay it with intention. What feels small today may one day shelter generations.

But bricks alone are not enough. You need God's fire to ignite vision and light the path ahead. As we step into the next chapter, *The Fire Your Future Depends On*, we will uncover how His fire draws us closer to the future He has uniquely designed for us.

## CHAPTER 3

# The Fire Your Future Depends On

*You call on the name of your god, and I will call on the name of the Lord. The god who answers by fire—he is God. 1 Kings 18:24 (NIV)*

*"The Holy Spirit can only fill a vessel that is empty, and He is waiting to fill us with fire. The fire of God never falls on dry wood; He falls on hearts that are ready and willing to burn."*
— Unknown[1]

### Where's the Fire?

In a small rural town, the fire department shared a line with the police. One morning, the chief of police was just clocking in when the phone rang. "Fire Department," he answered. A frantic voice shouted, *"Send the fire truck!"*, and then hung up. No details, no address, just an urgent cry and then silence.

Moments later, the phone rang again. "Fire Department!" The voice screamed, *"Send the fire truck!"* Click.

The phone rang a third time, and this time, he was ready. He quickly answered, *"Fire Department, where's the fire?"* The answer came back, *"In the kitchen!"*

This is how we often cry to heaven: *"Where is Your fire?"* We long for His presence, His flame, His power to consume our lives. We ache for revival, renewal, healing, for the miracles only His hand can bring.

While God never disconnects Himself from us, as this woman did, we often allow distractions to disconnect us from His presence and instruction. How often do we crave His power but resist the surrender that makes room for it? We want the flame, but hesitate to kneel at the altar where it burns. Without surrender, we drift into the probable, predictable, passionless, and safe. But when His fire falls, it propels us into the future He designed, alive with power and transformation.

## The Famine and the Silence

There is an episode in the book of Kings, where we find the nation of Israel in desperate need of that fire. After three years of severe famine, its land was cracked and barren. Streams turned to dust. Famine gnawed at their stomachs, and despair hung thick in the air.

Yet, the true famine was not in the fields, but in their hearts. The nation that once dedicated its lives and hearts to God had fallen away to the quiet deception of compromise. They still called on the LORD, but their devotion was divided. They longed for His blessings while dancing around the altars of idols. In their wavering, the heavens remained silent.

When hope seemed as far off as the rain, a lone voice pierced the stillness. Elijah, standing against the tide of spiritual indifference, called out to the nation, "How long will you waver between two opinions?" (1 Kings 18:21). The moment of choice had come, and with it, the opportunity for fire to fall.

## The Showdown Begins

The stage was set on Mount Carmel. The people gathered, their eyes fixed on the two altars, one surrounded by the 450 prophets of Baal, the other by one man, Elijah. The challenge was clear: "You call on the name of your god, and I will call on the name of the Lord. The god who answers by fire; He is God." (1 Kings 18:24).

The prophets of Baal began, calling on their god with fervor, dancing, shouting, and even cutting themselves in desperate pleas for a response. Hours passed, but there was no answer.

Their frenzy continued, but still, no fire came. Their performance, no matter how loud or frantic, could not produce the power of God. And before we judge them too quickly, we must recognize how often we do the same. We fill our lives with noise: activity, performance, and effort, believing it will move heaven. We pray for blessings without surrender, seek peace without repentance, and desire provision without aligning with God's will.

Then, it was Elijah's turn. With no theatrics and no frenzy, he stepped forward, quiet, yet confident in his God. Elijah had no need to strive; instead, he prayed. Before the crowd, he humbly rebuilt the altar of the Lord, reminding the people of their covenant with God. He took twelve stones and set the stage for something miraculous.

## The God Who Answers By Fire

Elijah then, "at the time of sacrifice", commanded the people to drench the altar with water, three times over, until it was soaked, leaving no room for doubt. Wet wood doesn't burn unless God sets it ablaze. What he was building wasn't just an altar; it was a stage for undeniable glory.

And that's exactly what happened. "At the time of sacrifice", with a simple, powerful prayer, he called on the Lord, saying, "Answer me, Lord, answer me, so these people will know that you, Lord, are God, and that you are turning their hearts back again." (1 Kings 18:37).

Then the fire fell.

Not a flicker, not a spark, but a consuming flame that devoured the sacrifice, the wood, the stones, and even the water in the trench. There was no room for doubt. This was the fire of God, holy, consuming, and undeniable. It left nothing untouched, no question unanswered.

This was the fire of affirmation, of holiness, of unmatched glory. God didn't just respond; He revealed Himself in a way no idol ever could. Because when God answers by fire, there's no room left for doubt.

## When Sacrifice Ignites the Fire

The fire didn't fall when the prophets of Baal danced, shouted, or whipped the crowd into a frenzy. A full day of performance couldn't produce what only God's presence can bring.

> **The fire fell on Elijah's sacrifice then, and it still falls on sacrifice today.**

What if we've mistaken volume for power, motion for devotion, emotion for encounter? Maybe the reason the fire hasn't fallen in our lives, homes, and churches is because we've traded surrender for performance. His fire doesn't fall on convenience, but on sacrifice.

And now we stand at the crossroad, where the heart of true worship and devotion is being lost. The question is not whether God still sends fire, but whether we have built an altar for it to fall on.

## God's Fire Doesn't Fall on Empty Altars

If you want the preferred future God has for you, you will need His fire. The future He has prepared isn't something you can build on human effort alone. It is bigger than your talent, greater than your resources, and beyond any strategy you can accomplish.

You need His power, His presence, and His purifying fire to shape you into the person that future requires. But God's fire doesn't fall on empty altars; it falls where something costly has been laid down.

Your preferred future will require sacrifice because it demands alignment with God's will, not your own. It means surrendering pride, letting go of control, and releasing plans that don't fit His purpose. I'm a witness that the fire still falls on sacrifice.

## When the Fire Fell for Me

One Sunday morning during a service, my pastor looked at the congregation and said, "The Lord says, there's one more person who's supposed to go on this mission trip to Zimbabwe." The moment those words left his mouth, I knew God was calling me. I just didn't know yet that it was an invitation to witness the God who answers by fire.

Honestly, I had every reason to say no. He and the other two team members had been planning this for months. Me? I had three weeks. Three weeks to prepare. Three weeks to raise money. Three weeks to get vaccinated, get a passport, and rearrange my entire life. And at that time, my life was already full.

My firstborn had just arrived, who was three weeks old when I said, "yes", and six weeks old when I left. I was teaching at a private Christian school, which meant no paycheck for the three weeks I'd be gone. And this would be the first time I had ever been separated from my wife. Everything in me wanted to stay comfortable.

Sacrifice was staring me in the face: my time, my resources, my family. But despite it all, I said yes. Why? Because sacrifice always costs something. And I had to be willing to lay it all down.

## The Fire Fell in Zimbabwe

When we arrived in Gweru, Zimbabwe, I saw the true cost of sacrifice. People walked for miles after long days of labor in the midst of famine. Some barefoot, some carrying babies, many with empty stomachs, yet all hungry for God. Not for lights or programs, but for His fire.

And the fire fell. I'll never forget the man with a cotton ball in his ear. As we prayed, it shot out, and he began shouting, "I can hear! I can hear!" The crowd erupted, and I stood in awe of God's power. I saw a wound close instantly and a man on the verge of cardiac arrest restored, but it was the deaf hearing that seared into my soul.

## The Fire Still Falls on Sacrifice

When I look back, that trip to Zimbabwe didn't just change them; it changed me. But it never would have happened without sacrifice. The sacrifice I made to go there, and the sacrifices they made to be in those meetings. They laid down what little they had just to encounter Him. Just as that encounter required sacrifice, so does the future God has designed for you.

## The Fire Your Future Depends On

The truth is, your preferred future, the one God designed for you, will cost you something too. Most people never experience their God-designed future, not because God hasn't prepared it, but because they aren't willing to lay down their own plans for His purpose. They cling to comfort, convenience, and control, while God is calling them to an altar of surrender.

I had to sacrifice my timing, my plans, and my vision for my life in order to step into what God was doing. And that principle still holds true: you can't walk into the future God has for you while holding on to the one you've planned for yourself. But let me share from my own experience. God's plan, His future for me, has far exceeded anything I could have imagined. And He wants to do the same for you.

After witnessing the healing of the man from cardiac arrest, I asked my pastor, "Why don't we see this in America?" He replied, "Because we have Tylenol, they don't." He was pointing out that we, as American believers, have grown comfortable with our material substitutes. We've traded altars for platforms, sacrifice for performance, and trust in God for trust in what we have or can purchase.

This shift has led us to a crossroads, where the heart of true worship and devotion is being lost. And it forces us to ask, what are we truly pursuing: applause or altars?

## The Cost of Performance Over Surrender

We've let compromise dim the flame. We endorse preachers and artists more for performance than purity, applauding style while ignoring lifestyle. Crowds fill churches and arenas, yet holiness goes wanting.

This isn't just their indictment; it's ours. Like Israel chasing Baal's show, we've built a culture of applause instead of altars. And we wonder why the fire doesn't fall.

Maybe the reason is this: We've traded holy sacrifices for hollow performances, lights and lingo for lives laid down. The fire hasn't fallen because surrender hasn't either. But when we yield, when we place our will on the altar, His fire burns brightest.

## The Hope That Ignites

The good news is this: God has not withdrawn His fire or abandoned His church. His glory has not changed. The darker the culture grows, the brighter His flame longs to burn through a surrendered people. When we return to the altar, trading performance for purity and pride for humility, His fire will fall again—refining, reviving, and empowering us for the future He has called us to build.

The God who answered by fire on Mount Carmel is the same God who answers today. His fire still falls on sacrifice, and when it does, everything changes.

Scripture repeats the pattern through Solomon dedicating the temple (2 Chronicles 7:1), David's offering on the threshing floor (I Chronicles 21:26), and the consuming of Gideon's gift (Judges 6:21). In the New Testament, believers prayed and were filled with fire (Acts 2), and at Calvary Jesus offered His life, raised by the Spirit's flame. Each story declares the same truth: God answers by fire.

But the fire does not fall on convenience or empty ritual. It falls on sacrifice. And every sacrifice requires an altar.

## Fire Follows Rebuilt Altars

Before the fire fell, Elijah did something we cannot overlook. He rebuilt the altar of the Lord that had been torn down (1 Kings 18:30).

The broken stones were more than rubble; they marked Israel's covenant with God, the place where obedience met devotion and offerings declared dependence on Him.

But Israel had abandoned it. In their drift toward Baal, the altar crumbled. Elijah knew that before fire could fall, the altar had to be restored. So he gathered twelve stones, one for each tribe, not just to call down fire but to restore their identity: You belong to Yahweh. You are His covenant people. Return to Him.

Revival does not begin with fire; it begins with rebuilding the altar. Could it be that we've lost our fire because we've abandoned the very place it was meant to fall?

## Four Futures, One Act of Surrender

Abraham's story is a tapestry of faith, each step drawing him closer to God's blueprint. He begins in Haran, settling into the safety of family and the familiar, a probable future shaped by comfort and predictability. Many of us settle there too, content with what feels secure, yet missing the larger destiny God has in store.

A famine drives him to Egypt, a plausible choice guided by reason, but not God's plan. Called back to the land of promise, Abraham learns that God's future cannot be built on human logic alone. Like him, we often cling to what seems practical, unaware that God is calling us beyond the safe and familiar.

Then comes the possible: the long-awaited birth of Isaac, a promise once thought impossible. Yet even this gift must be laid on the altar. In surrendering Isaac, Abraham releases not just his son but his vision of the future. That sacrifice opens the door to the preferred future; one only God could design.

## Access to a Heavenly Future

In that moment, Abraham is granted access to Heaven's vision, a future not just of fatherhood, but of fathering nations. His sacrifice brings forth a blessing beyond measure, a preferred future not just for him but for generations to come. He becomes the father of many, a legacy of faith built not on what he clung to, but on what he was willing to lay down.

> **His future for us far exceeds anything we could imagine or accomplish on our own.**

Abraham's journey shows us that while we may be tempted to settle for the probable or plausible paths, or even reach for the possible future, heaven's preferred future for our lives requires trust, surrender, and yes, sacrifice. To embrace God's plan, we must believe that.

And it's this surrender, this continual offering of ourselves, that fuels the fire God wants to ignite in us.

## Fire Fuels Vision

Fire is what fuels vision. Without it, leadership becomes nothing more than management, keeping things afloat at home, work, or church rather than breaking new ground and advancing toward the future God has planned.

It becomes about optics rather than outcomes, performance instead of presence. And that's why leaders are worn out; they're carrying loads God never asked them to carry alone. They're shouldering the weight of results without tapping into the One who produces true fruit. To them and to us, God gives this command: "The fire on the altar must be kept burning; it must not go out" (Leviticus 6:13)

The meetings you lead, the teams you manage, the ministry you build, none of it can thrive without His presence and power. And here's the question every leader needs to wrestle with: Are you leading on fumes or on fire?

You don't need another strategy session as much as you need an upper room experience. You don't need a better platform; you need a stronger altar. You don't need a bigger following; you need deeper surrender.

The preferred future God calls you to won't come through hustle alone; it comes through holy fire. It's not strategy or Spirit; it's both. But if you had to choose one, choose the fire. Start with the Spirit. Start with prayer. And trust me, that's coming from a "strategist".

## Ignite Your Leadership

Before you ask, *"What's the next big move?"* ask, *"Where's the fire?"* Because when you lose the fire, you lose more than energy; you lose clarity.

Fire is what lights the path forward when everything feels dark. Fire is what purifies your motives when selfish ambition tries to take over. Fire is what keeps your leadership humble and holy in a world that idolizes success.

This isn't just spiritual; it's leadership survival. Without fire, vision becomes vague, teams lose heart, and leaders default to control instead of trust. You start micromanaging instead of multiplying. You start protecting what you have instead of pursuing what God promised.

But when you have His fire, everything changes. Fire gives boldness when fear wants to shrink back. Fire gives resilience when pressure says to quit. Fire keeps you soft enough to love people and strong enough to lead them.

So, before you launch that next initiative, build that next plan, or step on that next stage, do what Elijah did—rebuild your altar. Invite the fire. Because leadership without fire isn't leadership; it's survival.

## 3 Practical Ways to Stay on Fire Without Burning Out

1. **Protect the Secret Place**. Your most important meeting isn't on your calendar; it's your time with God. Lead from overflow, not emptiness.
2. **Anchor in Identity, Not Outcomes**. Fire keeps you focused on who God says you are, not on metrics that rise and fall.
3. **Lead From Presence, Not Pressure**. Start every major decision on your knees before you stand before your team. When His fire leads, His wisdom flows.

But how do we position ourselves to receive that fire?

## How to Rebuild Your Altar Today

Return to prayer, not as routine but as a lifeline. Open your Bible, not for notes or captions, but for transformation. Let His Word shape your thoughts, values, and decisions. Restore worship, not as a playlist, but as a lifestyle of surrender.

Then recommit to sacrifice. Lay down pride, control, and timelines. Give God what costs you and remove the idols of: comfort, image, and ambition. You cannot rebuild the altar and keep your idols.

Where there is no altar, there is no sacrifice. Where there is no sacrifice, there is no fire. If you want the fire to fall, rebuild the altar and give Him something to consume. To move beyond the probable into the preferred, you need God's fire, and it only falls on sacrifice.

## When the Spirit Meets Your Yes

The future God has for you will not be fueled by effort alone but by His fire. And fire does not fall on empty altars; it falls on surrendered lives. The question is simple: what happens when His Spirit meets your yes?

In the next chapter, we'll explore *Unleashed Power*—what it means when the Spirit meets your surrender, transforming not just your plans but your life. The future God has promised won't be built by effort alone; it will require His authority.

# SECTION II

# The Past and the Power

(Chapters 4-5)

CHAPTER 4

# Unleashed Power—The Quiet Yes That Sparks Revival

*"Not by might nor by power, but by My Spirit," says the Lord Almighty.*
— Zechariah 4:6 (NIV)

*"When we work, we work. When we pray, God works."*[1]
— Hudson Taylor

### The Brick That Builds the Future

One afternoon, on a visit to the home of John Wesley, the 18th-century evangelist whose faith sparked revival, Billy Graham stepped off the bus and into a consecrated space. As the group moved from room to room, Graham lingered behind, drawn to a worn patch of wooden floor beneath a modest window.

This was no ordinary corner of the house. It was, in fact, the very spot where Wesley had knelt for hours, pouring out his soul in prayer and pleading with heaven for revival and renewal.

Once the tour ended, the tour group returned to the bus, only to discover Graham was not among them. After several minutes had passed, the group grew restless. Finally, the concerned guides sent someone back to find him.

They found him alone in that small room, knees pressed into those wooden notches, head bowed in prayer. And faintly, under his breath, he uttered a prayer that changed the world:

*"Oh Lord, do it again! Do it again."*[2]

This is the power of unleashed leadership: it turns ordinary people into instruments of the Master, igniting apathetic hearts and setting nations ablaze.

It does not come by chance and is not stumbled upon. It cannot be manufactured by efforts of will, charisma, or performance. It is unimpressed by privilege, prominence, or position.

It is the byproduct of rigorous prayer and proximity to the Holy God. It carries his power to break down strongholds, fortify families, and reshape history. It is the reward of the faithful, the enduring, and those who cling to the heart of God despite temptations to doubt, quit, or fall away.

## Do It Again, Lord: How Surrender Shapes Your Destiny

Billy Graham didn't become a world-changing evangelist in a single moment. And John Wesley didn't spark a revival overnight. Their unleashed power wasn't a flash of charisma or a surge of spotlight. It was forged in the furnace of prayer, refined in obscurity, and revealed over time.

The future isn't formed by chance but by prayer, purpose, and daily choices. Each one a seed. True power begins before vision shines or crowds gather. It starts in hidden places, in secret prayers, unseen tears, and faith that won't quit.

## The Trinity of Power

Three keys unlock the preferred future. I call them the "Trinity of Power". They give us the resolve to pursue God's future. Without them, we drift, disconnected from the very power He longs to release through us.

The first is **prayer**—**spiritual power.** Prayer is the builder's breath, the force that pulls heaven to earth. It doesn't just soothe; it aligns, sharpens, and strengthens. Before a stone is laid or a plan unfolds, prayer prepares the ground. Futures begin in the secret place, quiet, humble, powerful.

The second is **purpose**—**motivational power.** Purpose is the fire that sustains when work grows heavy and results come slow. It steadies your hands when doubts whisper. It reminds you not just of *what* you build, but *why*, and for whom. Conviction, not comfort, carries you forward.

The third is **choice**—**decisional power.** Choice is where obedience becomes movement, where your yes sets Heaven's design in motion. Every yes is a step from fear into alignment. Futures shift not by vision alone, but by the choices we dare to make.

These three, **Prayer, Purpose, and Choice**, form Heaven's blueprint for building destiny. Wielded together, they unleash a power no storm can undo.

## Power Source #1: Prayer —Where Futures Are Forged

We're often captivated by the moments that make headlines. We see the roar of the crowd, the spotlight of the stage, the sermon that goes viral, or the ministry that seems to blossom overnight. But those are not the beginning. They are the harvest of seeds planted long before they broach the surface; back when the only spotlight was the flicker of a candle during midnight prayers, and the only applause was the sound of heaven leaning in.

Before Nehemiah picked up a trowel, he wept in prayer. Before David faced Goliath, he wrestled a lion and a bear. Before Jesus stepped into public ministry, He endured the silence of the wilderness, forty days of hunger, resistance, and sacred resolve.

We must come to see hiddenness not as delay but as divine development. It is the holy furnace where endurance is formed and identity is clarified. It is the quiet rehearsal of destiny before stepping onto the stage of history.

## Strength in Stillness

God forms world-changers in obscurity before He reveals them in influence. The prison comes before the palace and the cross before the resurrection. So, if you feel hidden, unseen, or ordinary—rejoice! You're not forgotten, you are being forged.

No great move of God ever began without prayer. And no builder of families, churches, or legacies can build something that lasts without it. Prayer is the oxygen of construction, the thunder behind the whisper, the power behind every brick.

So how do you begin?

## A.CT.S.

One soul-shaping rhythm I've returned to often is the ancient pattern of ACTS: Adoration, Confession, Thanksgiving, and Supplication[3]. Adoration lifts your eyes, reminding your soul that He is holy, sovereign, and near. Confession clears the heart, unclenches the fists, and releases what you were never meant to carry. Thanksgiving turns your gaze from scarcity to abundance, from ache to awe. And Supplication opens the door, inviting heaven's power into earth's need.

This is prayer: not just words, but wonder. Not performance, but presence. It is the quiet place where builders are born and futures begin. It's how you breathe when you stand in a heap of rubble. It's spiritual oxygen for your soul, and one that can blow on embers of faith and kindle the fire that began your mission in the first place.

Because whatever you start without prayer, you'll have to sustain without God. And without His power, the walls may rise, but they will not endure.

Prayer is not the backup plan; it is the master plan. If prayer invites heaven into the blueprint, purpose ignites the reason you keep building.

## Power Source #2: Purpose — The Fire Behind the Build

Purpose fuels your "why", the God-given burden that burns deeper than applause and lasts longer than difficulty.

Simon Sinek popularized the phrase "Start with Why"[4], and though his message targeted business leaders, the principle is timeless and deeply biblical. Your "why" is not just a mission statement; it is the furnace of your endurance. It is what gives your actions staying power when the work is hard, the progress slow, and the applause absent.

Jesus Himself modeled this in John 4:34: "My food," said Jesus, "is to do the will of him who sent me and to finish his work." Christ's clarity of purpose gave Him strength for the wilderness, for Gethsemane, and for the cross. Purpose isn't a luxury; it's fuel.

Without knowing your "why," leadership becomes performance. Ministry becomes an obligation. Influence becomes image maintenance. But when you are clear on why you're building, on what vision

God has entrusted to you, you can keep laying bricks even when the scaffolding is bare and the night is long.

You're not just constructing a career or ministry. You're building a future. A refuge. A testimony. A legacy.

## Anchored by Purpose, Sustained by Fire

Between God's promise and its fulfillment, rough days will come, days that strike in ways you never imagined, enough to make you question everything. In those moments, you need more than platitudes on a wall. You don't need a vision statement; you need a vision anchor. That's what purpose is.

Purpose gives you the stamina to press on when you're tired and others say you've done enough. It wakes you at dawn to pray for dreams others dismissed. It is what roots you when criticism howls, when comparison tempts, and when results feel far away.

It keeps you steady in discomfort and guards you from drifting when progress feels out of reach. It gives you the strength to persevere when every bone in your body begs you to stop.

## Know Your *Why*

So, write it. Pray it. Revisit it. Breathe it. Because your *why* won't just provide a refuge for you when the storms come; it'll give others a reason to find shelter under your roof too. Purpose guards us from drift in the wilderness, like Israel, and sustains us against opposition, like David. It's why we sacrifice and pursue great instead of settling for good.

When your why is eternal, even the mundane becomes holy. This isn't about titles, but trust. Not applause, but assignment. You're not filling a slot; you're forming a path of grace others can walk through.

Your impact isn't defined by your role, but by your reason.

Leaders rarely falter from lack of skill; they falter when their fire dims under routine, criticism, and noise. Burnout doesn't come from the weight itself, but from losing sight of *why* we carry it.

That's why purpose matters. It doesn't just keep you from drifting; it fuels you to keep building when quitting feels easier. And history gives us living proof.

## For the Joy Set Before You

I remember visiting Mandela's prison cell on Robben Island, a small, barren space that whispered of unimaginable endurance. Later, I saw his home, walls still scarred by bullets from a regime that tried to silence him. And yet Mandela's why, freedom, justice, reconciliation, was so rooted that no prison could cage it and no weapon could destroy it. His purpose gave him the power to forgive where others would have chosen revenge.

Hebrews 12:2 whispers through the noise: "For the joy set before Him, He endured the cross…"

That was Jesus' why. The joy of redemption. The joy of resurrection. The joy of reunion. And it was enough.

So, what's the joy set before you? What vision wakes you up in the dark and won't let you go? What promise still stirs your soul even when the walls haven't risen? What's the vision that still burns quietly beneath the surface, even when no one else sees the flame?

## Power Source #3: Choice — The Yes That Builds the Future

It's not confusion that keeps us from choosing; it's the cross we sense behind the choice. Because the decisions we face aren't just tasks;

they're altars. And every altar demands a sacrifice: the tear of release, the ache of surrender, the silent resolve that follows obedience.

But here's the deeper truth: pain will find you either way. The real question isn't *if* you'll hurt; it's *how*. Will it be the pain of discipline or the ache of regret? One sanctifies. One steals. One carves character into your bones. The other slowly erodes your soul.

**Don't fear the pain that builds.** Fear the comfort that blinds. The discomfort of obedience is holy; it strips away the false, the fragile, and the fleeting. The pain of regret, though quieter, burrows deeper, haunting the chambers of what could've been.

So, choose your altar. Choose your pain. Only one leads to freedom. Only one is met by fire from heaven.

I've seen what happens when someone dares to choose a different future, one that's preferred, not predicted. One that requires sacrifice, releases legacy.

## The Altar of Decision: Where Obedience Becomes Legacy

My mother tried to quit smoking for years. The habit was deep, the craving relentless. Many attempts failed until a hospital stay and a diagnosis of emphysema changed everything. The doctor told her she had five years, maybe less, if she didn't quit. She was devastated.

Something holy ignited in her that day: a fire not of shame, but of clarity. She wanted to live, see her grandchildren grow, and leave more than memories behind.

We prayed. She got a patch. And after decades of smoking, she quit.

That choice didn't just add years; it birthed a legacy. She lived nearly twenty more years, saw her grandson married, led a senior home with wisdom and joy, and served as a deaconess for over a decade. Many still testify to her kindness, her servant's heart, and her steady presence.

Her decision extended her life and unleashed her calling. That's the power of one courageous yes. Like her, we hold the same power of choice, an invitation from heaven to join in what God is building.

## The Power of Choice: Heaven's Invitation in Your Hands

Prayer opens Heaven, but choice opens the door. You can carry vision in your heart, blueprints in your hand, and God's whisper in your ears, but nothing changes until you choose.

It's the holy intersection where divine prompting meets human participation. God won't force your hand, but He will anoint your feet if you move. He offers guidance, presence, and power, but you must still choose. Still build. Still act.

> **Choice is the hinge on which futures swing.**

Here lies the hidden miracle of transformation: your next future is one surrendered decision away. You didn't choose how your story began, but you do choose how it ends. As the saying goes, "You're born looking like your parents, but you die looking like your decisions."[5]

That's the weight, and the wonder, of free will. Every choice either builds toward the future God intended or buries it beneath the rubble of indecision.

## The Turning Point of Transformation

Adam and Eve's choice fractured a world. Jesus' choice in Gethsemane began its redemption. Choice is not small. It is God-given, and it is always yours to make.

We often wait for clarity, for a sign, for perfect timing. But in God's kingdom, change is less about timing and more about turning. You don't drift into wholeness; you turn toward it. You don't fall into freedom; you walk there, one decision at a time.

Noah built the ark.
Esther stood for her people.
Jesus surrendered in Gethsemane.

Each one, a choice.

Each choice seemed ordinary. Just another brick. But heaven knew. Legacy knew. Generations not yet born were watching. The future always turns on the hinge of courage.

And let's be clear: not choosing is also a choice. Passivity holds power too, the power to keep you circling the same mountain, bound by the same lies, while freedom waits at the door.

## The Choice Is Yours

Your calling isn't waiting for certainty; it's waiting for surrender. Forgive, stay faithful, return, risk, rest; each choice is power, each yes a seed of freedom.

> **When you choose in alignment with heaven, hell trembles, futures shift, history bends.**

God blesses not just the outcome but the moment of choosing. Heaven leans in when you whisper, "Here I am." Even when resources are low, the path unclear or your hands shaking, you can still choose.

So, what's in your hands today: a habit to break, a call to make, a prayer to pray, a dream to revive? Choose. Because the future isn't found; it's built. And building begins with a decision.

Scripture shows us the same truth in Paul's story.

## The Power of Choice and Your Preferred Future

One Spirit-led choice altered the trajectory of the early Church. That's the power of the Preferred Future: it whispers beneath the noise, inviting you to trade comfort for calling, familiarity for faith, and when you say "yes", Heaven moves.

Paul had a plan. His goal was to enter Bithynia, an option that seemed reasonable, even strategic for the gospel. Had he gone, it would have been his *possible future*—driven by intention, vision, and his desire to spread the gospel. But the Spirit of Jesus said "no." Heaven closed the door. Not because Bithynia was wrong, but because Macedonia was *right*.

Macedonia wasn't just possible; it was *preferred*. A woman named Lydia, a riverside prayer meeting, and a gospel movement that would ripple across Europe, all hinged on Paul choosing not what was available, but what was *appointed*.

That's the power of Spirit-led surrender: the choice to trade what's good for what's God.

You might be standing at an open door that looks logical, profitable, or even admirable. But is it *God's* door? Or are you preparing to build in Bithynia while your miracle is waiting in Macedonia?

This is why leaders in ministry, parenting, marriage, or business need more than smart strategies. You need spiritual sensitivity. Discernment is found in stillness. Born in the quiet, sharpened in prayer, anchored in purpose, and confirmed through obedient choice. That's where prayer, purpose, and choice converge.

## When All Three Converge

If you pray and know your why but never choose…you'll stay inspired, but stuck. If you know your why and choose but never pray…you'll move, but without direction. If you pray and choose but lack a clear why…you'll act, but without endurance.

But when all three converge, prayer, purpose, and choice, you don't just build with passion. You build with power. That's when your life begins to echo beyond the moment. That's when the future you were born for begins to rise.

We see it in Nehemiah's story.

## The Future You Were Born For

Nehemiah was an exiled cupbearer with a burden burning brighter than his position. When he heard Jerusalem's walls lay in ruins, he didn't rush to fix them. He wept, fasted, and prayed, and in that stillness, God shaped him with a shepherd's purpose, a builder's grit, and a warrior's resilience.

Opposition soon came. Sanballat mocked. Tobiah threatened. Fear whispered. But Nehemiah made a choice: *"I am doing a great work, and I cannot come down"* (Nehemiah 6:3). He built with one hand and warred with the other.

The wall rose in 52 days, but the greater miracle was revival in the people. Nehemiah's private surrender became their public strength. And that kind of revival is still forged the same way, through leaders who pray, who remember their purpose, and who choose obedience when quitting would be easier.

Generations may change, but God's blueprint does not. What built walls in Jerusalem and launched the gospel in Macedonia is the same blueprint that builds churches, families, and legacies today. I saw it happen in Atlanta.

## A 40-Day Turning Point

A mid-sized church outside Atlanta was losing momentum. Worship was good. Preaching was solid. But the energy felt flat, engagement was slipping, and staff were exhausted. They didn't need another five-year plan; they needed a reset.

So they tried something simple: forty days of focus. Every ministry, every small group, every sermon leaned into one theme. People prayed together, shared where they'd seen God at work, and asked what step He was calling them to take.

At first, the shift felt small. But soon something stirred. People lingered after service. Teams prayed without prompting. Volunteers stepped forward, not because of polished pitches, but because God was moving.

The fruit of those forty days lasted for decades. Committed disciples. Vibrant groups. Rekindled callings. A culture alive with God's presence.

I know, because that church is the one I pastor.

This is how a church finds its future, not by chasing the next big thing, but by returning to the small things that matter most.

What we found in Atlanta is what God has shown throughout Scripture: forty days often mark a turning point.

## Unleash: A 40-Day Invitation

Throughout Scripture, 40 days mark divine turning points. Forty days of rain prepared Noah to rebuild. Forty days on Sinai prepared Moses to lead with glory. Forty days in the wilderness prepared Jesus to step into purpose.

God often uses 40 days not as a pause, but as preparation for something new to begin.

That's what the Unleash 40-Day Future Shift Devotional invites you into, not a sprint, but a rhythm. A daily return to the work of partnering with God as He builds the future He's promised. Not by force. Not by frenzy. But by faith.

These 40 days are about more than a devotional. They're an invitation to practice faithfulness. To take small, steady steps toward the future God is calling you to. Not grand gestures, but consistent devotion.

The future you've glimpsed, the family culture you long for, the impact you hope to make, the soul-deep fulfillment you've nearly given up on will not happen all at once. It will be built one prayer at a time. One choice. One boundary. One conversation. One act of courage.

Download the *Unleash* 40-Day Future Shift Devotional at www.donbrawley.com/unleash or scan **QR Code below.**

## You're Invited

Accept the invitation. Let these 40 days shape not just your schedule but your soul. Show up with intention, even in small ways, and everything shifts: atmosphere, courage, hope. Not because you know it all, but because you dared to begin.

You are not powerless. Even if you feel overwhelmed or have failed before, you still hold the power to pray again, to lead again, to believe again. God rarely lights the whole path; He illuminates the next step. And that step begins with a choice.

Prayer, purpose, and choice set the future in motion, but you cannot step into it while chained to yesterday. To rise with God's promise, you must first break free. And that's where we turn in the next chapter.

## CHAPTER 5

# Break Free for a New Future

*"Do not conform to the pattern of this world, but be transformed by the renewing of your mind."*
— Romans 12:2 (NIV)

*"Our past may explain us, but it doesn't excuse us. Ultimately, we are responsible for who we become."*[1]
— John Ortberg

### The Past Isn't a Chain—Unless You Let It Be

I remember sitting in a leadership meeting one Monday night, nodding along, offering insight, doing what leaders do. But beneath the surface, I wasn't really there. Just days earlier, I had run into someone who had left our church years ago. There was no conversation, no closure, just a knowing look, and then they were gone again. The encounter didn't leave me angry, but it did awaken a dull ache I thought I'd laid to rest years ago.

So I sat there in my meeting, doing my best to lead, while an old and uninvited voice whispered beneath the surface: *Maybe you're not cut out for this. It's only a matter of time until you'll fail them, too.*

Like every good lie, its voice sounded like my own. It wasn't long before it had me questioning why I thought I could lead in the first place.

I've spoken with enough leaders to know these experiences are not unique to me. Many of us have faced similar dilemmas; moments where we must be outwardly composed and confident, while fighting a silent war most people will never know about.

Oftentimes, it's not others' opinions that shackle us but the residues of our pasts. That forgiven mistake that you can't forget. That wound that never fully healed. That season you survived…but just barely.

> **Unfortunately, we can be called, capable, and still chained.**

Even free on the outside, we can be bound within. And that bondage doesn't just affect us; it affects those we lead, because you can't lead others into freedom when your own hands are still bound in chains.

You can't heal what you hide, and you can't outgrow what you won't name.

## Recognizing the Chains of the Past

Many of us underestimate the grip of the past because we've learned to manage it. We bury it beneath busyness, mask it with success, or cover it with spiritual clichés like, "I'm blessed and highly favored," even when it couldn't feel farther from the truth.

But make no mistake—your past still speaks. It shows up in your patterns, your assumptions, your silence, and your striving. If left unchecked, it will quietly co-author your future.

The past may feel like an anchor, but it doesn't have to hold you back. Every step of faith loosens the chains and begins a new story. But before you can rewrite that story, you must first recognize how loudly the old one still echoes.

## The Mental Weight of History

Let's imagine for a moment that you are leading a growing team. The engagement is high, the vision is palpable, but then, someone raises a simple question in a meeting. They second-guess a process or find a flaw in your reasoning. Though there are no ill intentions in their question, that doesn't stop it from landing like a pile of bricks.

A memory surfaces: a time your voice was dismissed, your presence overlooked, or your value was questioned. And now suddenly, you're no longer defending a strategy; you're defending your worth. Instead of leading from clarity, you are leading from a wound.

## When Pain Becomes a Pattern

These are the hidden chains, not on your wrists, but in your thoughts. Experiences become assumptions. Assumptions harden into strongholds. And those strongholds begin to shape how we see ourselves, our calling, and the future we believe we're allowed to have.

Too often, we live as if our story is already written, stuck in cycles of fear or shame that feel permanent.

Sometimes, those stories sound like this:

- "It's too late for me to start again."
- "I don't deserve a second chance."
- "This is just how it is for people like me."

And here's the wild part: those voices *feel* true. But they're **not** the truth; they are *echoes*. Echoes of unhealed moments, unnamed fears, and lies we never challenged.

They're not facts; they're stories, narratives we've rehearsed for so long. Like ivy creeping over stone, they slowly entangle our minds until we forget what freedom was ever supposed to feel like.

But those inner narratives are not destiny. And if the future isn't fixed in stone, then your mindset shouldn't be either, because an unfixed future requires a growth mindset, not a fixed one. But that doesn't come without a fight.

## When the Mind Becomes a Battleground

In cognitive psychology, recurring false mental scripts are called ANTs—Automatic Negative Thoughts,[2] a term coined by Dr. Daniel Amen. These are the quiet reflexes that surface when life brushes up against old pain. They're persistent, subconscious, and often rooted in wounds that never fully healed.

You get passed over for a promotion, and your mind whispers, "You never measure up." Someone leaves your church without a word, and your heart absorbs, "You're a failure." You miss a moment at home, and hear, "You've dropped the ball. Again."

These aren't just fleeting thoughts; they become beliefs. And those beliefs begin to shape how you interpret new opportunities, navigate relationships, and confront challenges. Instead of filtering life through truth, you start seeing it through the shadow of your past.

And those beliefs shout louder after you've been triggered.

## Freedom: An External State or an Internal Reality?

Triggers are rarely random. Something small: a glance, tone, or delay can unleash a cascade of buried lies. Like a Trojan Horse, the ANTs of your mind ride in on the back of unresolved pain, using your vulnerability to reinforce trauma instead of truth.

But every trigger is a crossroads: Will you bow to the old story or challenge it with truth? Will you rehearse the wound or reframe what God is redeeming?

That's why two people can face the same moment and respond completely differently. One sees rejection while the other sees growth; one braces for failure while the other steps forward in faith. The difference isn't what happened; it's what they believed about what happened.

The stories we believe don't just shape our perspective; they shape our alignment.

Because what you believe determines what you build. When your heart aligns with truth, your decisions gain clarity, your direction sharpens, and your leadership flows from purpose, not pressure.

I've seen it in leaders across ministry, business, and family life. Even when we're free on the outside, we can still be captive on the inside.

And Scripture gives us a vivid example of this inner captivity.

## Letting Go: The Path to Freedom

God had finally delivered the Children of Israel, the Red Sea had been split in two, and Pharaoh and his army were defeated. Freedom had come at last. But freedom isn't just about walking out of a place; it's about leaving behind the mindset that bound you.

And their mindset hadn't caught up.

So when discomfort came, they grumbled, "We should've stayed in Egypt. At least there we had meat" (Exodus 16: 2–3, paraphrased).

They experienced a supernatural deliverance; yet they were still mentally tethered to Egypt.

They weren't in chains anymore, but their thoughts were. That's the power of an unhealed past; you can break free outwardly and still think like a captive. Even called, gifted, anointed leaders quietly wrestle with 'not enough.'

And you're not alone.

## Healing What You Can't Carry Forward

If you've led long enough, you carry scars. Some are visible. Others are tucked behind titles, responsibilities, and roles.

Maybe you've carried others' needs so long, you forgot your own. Maybe you lost someone and never fully grieved. Perhaps you compromised to keep the peace and lost sight of yourself. Maybe you were overlooked, and now you overcompensate. You've survived betrayal and promised never to trust again. Or perhaps you failed publicly and vowed never to risk again.

You're not weak. You're human. But what you don't name, you can't release. And what you refuse to release will quietly shape your future. Awareness is the beginning, not the end.

There comes a moment in every builder's life when you realize: You can't carry everything into the future God is calling you to build.

Not every memory. Not every failure. Not every relationship. Not every wound.

Some things must be released, not because they weren't real, but because their work is done.

To be clear, letting go is not the same as denial. It's not minimizing the pain or pretending it didn't happen. It's the courageous act of releasing what no longer belongs in your future. And that healing work often begins with one uncomfortable word: forgiveness.

## Forgiveness Is a Weapon, Not a Weakness

Unforgiveness is like running a marathon while dragging a suitcase full of bricks. You might think you can keep going, preaching, parenting, and leading, but eventually, the weight wears you down. And sooner or later, it seeps into everything: your joy, your decisions, your relationships, even your vision for the future.

Many leaders carry old pain into new seasons; not from enemies, but from the places they thought were safe. Our deepest cuts rarely come from strangers. They come from parents who never affirmed us, from family members who failed to see or support us, from friends who didn't show up, and from mentors who misused their influence. The list goes on.

I've lived it. I've stood in the pulpit preaching hope with a bleeding heart. I've trusted voices that turned on me. I've poured into people who later stood against me. And it broke me; but it didn't bury me. Because even in the breaking, God was working.

And the hurt the enemy used as a lie, God began to uncover with truth.

## Freedom from The Lies

God delivered me from the lie that every departure was a rejection.

For years, I carried each goodbye like a quiet question: *Do I have what it takes to keep going without them?*

Maybe I didn't have enough.
Enough strength.

Enough support.
Enough wind left in my lungs to keep building.

Or worse…maybe *I* wasn't enough.

But then I saw it.
I wasn't abandoned.
I was *entrusted*.

That was the paradigm shift, and suddenly I understood:

What felt like subtraction was God creating room for addition. He wasn't taking people from me, but lifting the weight of those who couldn't travel where I was going.

What felt like rejection was really redirection. He removed the voices that distracted me from hearing Him clearly.

What felt like loss was really a clearing, making room for stronger seeds, deeper roots, and a harvest yet to come.

## Released to Build Again

Sometimes the ground has to be cleared before new life can grow. And sometimes, what walks away is not evidence of your failure; it's evidence of God's faithfulness making room for what's next.

Growth didn't come through gaining more but through releasing what no longer belonged. And I had to let go, not just of people, but of unmet expectations, unspoken wounds, and the silent fears that still whispered in the dark.

Forgiveness isn't just about settling the past; it's about reclaiming the future. It's the fearless decision to say, "Not this way," and to build forward with freedom, not baggage.

It doesn't excuse the offense; it breaks its grip. It's not about forgetting; it's about choosing to stop bleeding. It's the courageous decision to say, "*You don't get to define me. You don't get to narrate my future. I'm not staying stuck; I'm stepping forward.*"

And sometimes, the person you most need to forgive is yourself, for that missed opportunity, that choice you regret, that season you went numb, that failure you keep replaying, wondering if it's disqualified you.

You can carry guilt like a badge, hoping it might somehow redeem what was lost. But guilt doesn't redeem; it only repeats. To truly break free, you must release them and release yourself.

## Released to Rise

Before he became the Church's greatest apostle, Paul was its fiercest persecutor: approving executions, hunting down believers, and throwing them in jail. If anyone had a past that could disqualify him, it was Paul. Yet in Philippians 3:13-14, he writes, "Forgetting what is behind and straining toward what is ahead, I press on…"

Forgetting doesn't mean erasing; it means refusing to let the past define the future. Paul didn't deny his past; he reframed it. It became context, not a cage. Fuel, not failure.

> **The past may explain you, but it doesn't get to define you.**

That's our invitation, too, to stop letting what was steal what could be.

Because when we look closely, regret often wears a familiar face.

If you're a parent juggling work, church, and family, maybe the regret isn't about others; it's about the time you've lost. The chances you didn't take. The years you can't get back.

But whatever your story, it doesn't have to write your next chapter.

You are more than what was done to you, more than what you've done, more than the season you barely survived.

And if you ever doubt it—look at the cross.

## Pain Doesn't Get the Final Word

The cross is proof that your worth isn't tied to your wounds, and your future isn't canceled by your past. But to live in that truth, something must be released: the hurts that still haunt, the labels that still linger, the lies that still whisper.

You may not be able to change the past, but you can change how you interpret it, how you carry it, and what you build from it. Your story isn't set in stone; it's shaped by the meaning you attach to it.

Your past is like stained glass, thousands of broken pieces and mismatched shards. But when God's truth shines through, and grace becomes your lens, those fragments become something breathtaking.

Pain doesn't get the final word. Perspective does. That's what Joseph discovered when he stood before his brothers and declared, *'What you meant for evil, God meant for good'* (Genesis 50:20). That's the power of redemption; it doesn't discard the pieces; it rearranges them with purpose.

To live in that redemption, you must confront the old scripts still shaping your life. That's why we must rewrite the stories we tell ourselves.

## The Stories That Shape Us

Picture a young elephant, born into the noise of the circus. At its birth, it's clasped with a chain, its leg bound to a heavy stake with thick iron links. Instinctually, it pulls, thrashes, and resists, but the chain holds. Over time, the elephant grows strong and majestic; all the while the chain is made smaller and smaller until it is ultimately replaced by a thin rope. Still, the elephant stays. Not because the rope is stronger, but because the story is.

Somewhere along the way, it stopped resisting. It accepted a lie: "This is all I'll ever be." And with that lie, its freedom and its future are decided, not by a rope or trainer, but by a belief.

And you and I? We're not so different.

We walk with open gates behind us, yet live like prisoners, tethered not by chains, but by unchallenged chapters. We confuse comfort with calling, survival with significance, and stability with purpose.

That's the danger of routine becoming a cage. It's when we as leaders preach freedom while quietly carrying shame. It's when we exhort others to step boldly into new seasons while still fearing the pain of our last.

Some chains don't rattle; they blend into our sermons, schedules, and smiles, but they weigh on us just the same.

## Rewriting the Stories We Tell Ourselves

You weren't created to live within the limits others have placed on you.

You were formed in the image of a God who sees not just your *probable* future, but your *preferred* one. He sees not just what is likely to happen, but what *should*, if you dare to believe it. But belief alone isn't enough. To live that future, you must rewrite the story.

In *Unlocking Leadership Mindtraps*, Jennifer Garvey Berger warns of our tendency to cling to "simple stories"—quick explanations that ease our uncertainty but distort reality[3]. We assume:

- He didn't text back—he must not respect me.
- They left the church—it was probably that sermon.
- My kid pulled away—it's because I failed them.
- She walked by without speaking—she must not like me.

These stories feel true, but they're often rooted in old wounds, not present truth. And in church life, we sometimes spiritualize them, calling it "discernment" when it's really fear. These aren't God's voice; they're simple stories, echoes of insecurity disguised as insight.

## Simple Stories

Simple stories are the one-dimensional narratives we tell ourselves to make sense of complex experiences. Berger explains that these simple stories give us a false sense of control and, therefore, limit our ability to grow and engage with complexity. These stories simplify reality, yet in doing so, they often trap us in limiting beliefs that prevent us from fully stepping into the freedom and growth God desires for us.

Consider these:

- A mother still hears the shaming voice of her ex-husband and quietly believes she'll never be worthy of respect.
- A father working long hours assumes emotional absence is the cost of providing and thinks to himself this is just what it takes to be a man.
- A leader, betrayed by her team, now leads with guardedness, convinced it's safer not to trust again.
- A business owner, once burned by failure, stops dreaming, telling himself, "I'm just not cut out for risk."

These stories may be anchored in the past, but they're far from buried.

## When Silence Isn't Healing

Simple stories aren't just echoes of where we've been; they become architects of where we're going. They echo through our choices, shaping the future we walk into.

This is why the Four Futures framework matters, not just as a theory, but as a mirror. Old stories drag us toward the probable future. But rewriting those stories opens the way to the preferred future God is calling us to build.

## Rewrite the Story, Rebuild the Future

When you rewrite the stories, you tell yourself, you break free from old narratives and step into new possibilities marked by growth, freedom, and purpose.

Stories rooted in fear or scarcity limit vision, dull courage, and disguise themselves as truth. But the cycle breaks the moment you name the lie, challenge it, and, by God's grace, rewrite it.

Transformation doesn't come by wishful thinking but by a renewed mind and surrendered heart (Romans 12:1-2). What you believe in private becomes what you build in public. Your inner story is the architect of your outer world, shaping how you love, lead, and live.

But if the architect is compromised, not by truth but by echoes, your future will be too. And those echoes often have names, voices that sound convincing but keep us stuck.

## The Voices That Keep You Stuck

Sometimes the stories we carry don't sound like lies. They sound like authority. They don't shout; they whisper. And those whispers shape us.

You've likely heard the voice of:

- **The Worrier** — always imagining worst-case scenarios. *"What if it all falls apart?*
- **The Judge** — rigid and merciless, constantly measuring you against perfection. *"You should be further along by now."*
- **The Critic** — fixated on your flaws. *"You never get it right."*
- **The Pessimist** — fatalistic and final, painting every setback as permanent. *"This always happens to you." "You'll never change." "No one really cares."*
- **The Imposter** — whispers that you don't belong and will be exposed. *"Any day now they'll realize you're a fraud."*
- **The Comparer** — constantly measuring your worth against others. *"Look at them; you'll never measure up."*

These voices are old. Some are inherited. Some were born in trauma. All of them feel familiar; they've echoed long enough to sound like you. But they're not the voice of your Father.

They are distortions, not direction. Accusations, not alignment.

And here's the danger: if you don't recognize the voice, you'll follow it. You'll confuse criticism for conviction, noise for discernment, and fear for wisdom.

You were made for the voice of the Spirit, truth in love, identity in grace, and hope whispered into your brokenness.

I've walked with hundreds of leaders: corporate executives, pastors, lay leaders, and entrepreneurs, helping them confront the voices that kept them stuck until they could hear another—the voice of redemption. That voice didn't just free them; it led them into futures they once thought impossible.

That's why in the *Unleash* **Masterclass**, we name these voices, trace their roots, and replace them with truth so you can live unleashed and lead from freedom—not fear.

*But you don't have to wait.*

You don't have to wait for your story to change; you can begin reframing it now. Start by naming the narrative you've been carrying, challenging it with truth, and replacing it with redemption. In the *Unleash* **Masterclass**, I walk leaders step by step through this process, but even here, these small shifts can open the door to freedom.

Next, we'll explore how to steward what's yours and release what isn't. It's time to unleash your leadership.

SECTION III

# Live with Vision. Lead with Fire

(Chapters 6-7)

## CHAPTER 6

# Unleash the Leader Within

*And David shepherded them with integrity of heart; with skillful hands he led them.*
— Psalm 78:72 (NIV)

*"Before you are a leader, success is all about growing yourself. When you become a leader, success is all about growing others."*[1]
— Jack Welch

### Before the Applause: The Formation of a Leader

Before the world called him a hero…before his name became a symbol of freedom…Nelson Mandela sat alone in a prison cell, forgotten and confined, cut off from the very movement he helped ignite. It was there that Mandela made a choice every great leader must make: he chose to lead himself before ever leading a nation.

He trained his mind to stay sharp and guarded his heart from hatred. He mastered his emotions, knowing that one day, his people would need more than a free man; they would need a formed man.

When I saw how narrow and bare his cell truly was, I felt more than the pressure of confinement. I felt the formative power being cultivated in that small space, and I was reminded that greatness isn't forged in comfort; it is shaped in the shadows, away from the applause.

## Leading in the Shadows

Mandela didn't wait for the spotlight to lead. He embraced the darkness as a place of becoming, letting the silence shape him, the waiting refine him, and the pain prepare him for the weight he was born to carry. When the gates finally opened, it wouldn't be just a free man walking out, but a ready one.[2]

And maybe you're not on Robben Island, but you know what it feels like to wait. To be delayed. Overlooked. Confined by a season you didn't choose.

What if this isn't a setback, but a divine forge? What if God is preparing you, not just to walk free, but to lead free?

The world doesn't just need gifted leaders; it needs whole ones. It's not something that comes from the spotlight, but must be formed in the quiet, in the space just small enough for you and God.

So, if you're in a season of obscurity, delay, or silence, don't despise it. Lean in, because the kind of leadership that transforms others starts when we learn to lead ourselves.

Hear me on this: Effective leadership begins with self-leadership.

## Before You Can Lead Outwardly, You Must Lead Within

By self-leadership, I don't mean trendy hacks or self-care tips. I mean soul work. The courage to face the one person you cannot outrun. To bring to your inner life the same devotion you pour into your work, roles, and duties.

It requires honesty about your motives, awareness of your patterns, stewardship of your energy and courage with your fears. It's learning to coach yourself before you try to lead anyone else.

When your soul is aligned, your leadership flows with integrity, but when it's fractured, your influence leaks, quietly at first, and then visibly.

Jesus gave us a great model to follow. Before stepping into public ministry, He was led into the wilderness (Luke 4:1–2) in preparation for His calling.

He went willingly into a period of testing, away from the noise of public opinion. He fought against temptation with valor and aligned with the Father. And only after this period did He step into His public assignment.

This wasn't incidental; it was intentional. A blueprint for all of us: you cannot bypass inner alignment on your way to outer impact.

And that alignment? It begins with clarity.

## The Foundations of Unleashed Leadership

Lasting influence doesn't begin with charisma or credentials. It begins with something deeper: internal clarity, emotional honesty, and spiritual discipline. These are the foundations of unleashed leadership.

### 1. Clarity Before Strategy

Great leadership doesn't begin with great plans; it begins with a clear identity. You can have sharp systems and a brilliant team, but if you don't know who you are, what you value, or what God is asking of you, you'll lead from confusion rather than conviction.

Clarity isn't a one-time revelation; it's a continual rhythm. It's formed in stillness, not busyness. In presence, not performance. In surrender, not striving. It's the quiet knowing that emerges when your soul sits still long enough to hear the whisper of the Spirit.

Clarity asks:

- What truly matters in this season, and am I giving it my best attention?
- What story am I believing, and is it even true?
- Where have I drifted, and how can I realign?

These are more than reflections; they are holy recalibrations. They realign your heart with your assignment. They strip away the noise and bring you back to the center. And when clarity takes root, it doesn't just clear confusion; it creates space for something even deeper to grow—honesty.

**2. Honesty**

Honesty is the soil where trust takes root. It is the courage to name the cracks in our souls, to bring shadows into the light, not for shame, but for freedom.

David wept and repented without reservation. Paul confessed his weakness with bold humility. These weren't moments of failure; they were doorways to deeper strength.

For leaders, honesty isn't a liability; it's liberation. It breaks down walls, deepens connection, and makes space for grace to breathe. But the hardest person to lead is often the one in the mirror. If you won't tell yourself the truth, your leadership will always carry a limp, even if no one else sees it.

I once worked with a leader who had built a large and respected organization. Years earlier, he engaged in an inappropriate relationship with a consenting adult, and when the truth came out, the media was relentless. Many in his position would have hidden, denied, or deflected. Instead, he chose the harder road. He confessed, submitted to a process of restoration, and walked it out with humility and integrity.

His transparency didn't erase the past, but it redeemed it. His humility turned a season of shame into a testimony of grace. And his integrity continues to impact me far more than his success ever did.

Honesty asks, "Is my identity rooted in my roles or in Christ?"

David's ancient prayer still echoes through time: "Search me, O God, and know my heart..." (Psalm 139: 23). Honesty with God brings you back to yourself. And when you're aligned within, you can lead with clarity, strength, and trust.

Once honesty is established, you can cultivate spiritual discipline, a rhythm that restores your soul and sustains your leadership through every season.

### 3. Spiritual Discipline

Spiritual discipline is the quiet engine of lasting leadership. Practices like prayer, worship, fasting, and journaling aren't just habits; they are lifelines. When clarity fades and strength runs thin, these rhythms anchor your soul and sustain your leadership.

They ask one question: *Am I making space to connect with God consistently?* Because without discipline, leadership withers. With it, every burden becomes an altar and every challenge a meeting place with Him.

And to lead well, you must steward the vessel, your energy, emotions, and your whole self. Influence doesn't flow from skill alone but from a heart aligned with Heaven's intention. That alignment begins not with more time, but with renewed strength and rhythms that restore what leadership withdraws.

## Leading from Overflow, Not Overwhelm

The real danger in leadership isn't collapse in a moment; it's erosion over time. Little by little, you trade renewal for routine, calling exhaustion 'normal' and mistaking busyness for faithfulness. You're still showing up, but no longer showing up full. Leading from overwhelm looks like nagging unrest, frayed patience, stifled creativity.

You may master the optics of producing on empty, but results without renewal always demand a price; what once flowed like a river becomes dammed.

Leading from overflow is different: it honors the secret place, draws strength before the day begins, and finds power not in doing more but in receiving more: more presence, more grace, more clarity, more of God.

## Overflow: The Fuel of Unleashed Leadership

Overflow doesn't begin with your calendar; it begins with your cup.

David had more reasons than most of us to look for affirmation in his accomplishments. King of a thriving nation, he expanded its borders and preparations for the temple to be built. But the pride of his leadership was anchored not in his accomplishments but in the depth of his encounters with God. He found a secret reservoir where his soul could be nourished despite the busyness of running a kingdom. That's why in Psalm 23 he says, *"You anoint my head with oil; my cup overflows."*

He understood that unleashed leadership is an outpouring of a soul that's been with God. Overflow isn't about listening to more podcasts, adding more to your planner, or finding a new productivity hack. Rather, it's the evidence of quiet integrity that finds its roots in God.

I know this the hard way. There was a season when I was doing so much, leading meetings, building teams, writing sermons, traveling, counselling, yet my soul was running on empty. I was producing, but I wasn't replenishing. I mistook adrenaline for anointing and ended up running on fumes.

The truth hit me in the quiet moments: I wasn't leading from overflow, I was leading from depletion. And depletion eventually demands a price. My patience was thinner, my creativity dulled, and my connection with God felt more functional than intimate.

That was the breaking point when I finally realized what David already knew: *true leadership cannot flow from exhaustion. It has to flow from God's presence.*

So I slowed down. I began returning to the secret place, not as another duty, but as a lifeline. I relearned how to abide before I attempted to achieve, how to rest before I led, how to let His presence refill what leadership was constantly draining.

That's the difference between burnout and breakthrough. And overflow is always cultivated in quiet places with God.

Each day demands an answer: am I leading from adrenaline or abiding in God's strength?

> **Burnout comes when you're running on empty; breakthrough comes when you're running on overflow.**

## Overflow Is Cultivated in Quiet Places

Overflow isn't found at the bottom of your inbox or by pushing harder, staying later, or adding one more thing. Jesus showed us the way: 'But Jesus often withdrew to lonely places and prayed' (Luke 5:16).

He didn't retreat because He was overwhelmed, but to stay aligned, anchored in the Father's presence, fueled by intimacy, not activity. We need that same rhythm. Especially as parents, pastors, and leaders called to carry others.

As one pastor confessed to me, 'I realized I'd been doing everything for God, and almost nothing with God.' That's the quiet drift we all face. Burnout doesn't come from a full calendar; it comes from misaligned focus. The invitation of overflow isn't to quit your responsibilities; it's to reclaim your connection.

The difference between burnout and breakthrough won't be in your workload; it'll be in your posture. Overflow doesn't begin with time management; it begins with soul surrender.

## From Overwhelmed to Overflowing: The Shift

Overflow is more than margin: it's a mindset, a Spirit-led shift in how you live, lead, and respond.

Here's what that shift looks like:

- Overwhelm says, "I have to keep up."
  Overflow says, "I have nothing to prove and only God to please."

- Overwhelm asks, "How much more can I carry?"
  Overflow asks, "What's mine to carry and what's not?"

- Overwhelm strives.
  Overflow abides. (*John 15:5*)

Overflow won't just change your pace; it'll radically transform your presence. Your edges will become softer, and your meetings more impactful. Where your leadership was grounded in grind, it will root in the steady comfort of grace.

Your family will feel different. Your work will feel different. Your church will feel different. And most importantly, *you* will feel different.

Because you're not just leading from clarity but communion, and when communion is your *lifeline*, everything else is in overflow. You won't have to force your leadership; it'll simply flow.

But even when we're full, there's still another trap we must confront: the subtle temptation to take back the reins.

## Influence Over Control

Control wears many disguises, excellence, urgency, even "just trying to help", but beneath it all is fear masquerading as leadership. It promises peace but only multiplies pressure. The tighter you grip, the heavier the burden becomes, until you're carrying weights God never asked you to hold.

Jesus showed us a better way. He chose twelve imperfect disciples, walked with them, corrected them, and then released them. His words still ring true: *"You will do even greater things…"* (John 14:12). Influence multiplies when you empower, not when you control.

Letting go is hard. It feels like risk, but Proverbs 3:5 reminds us: *"Trust in the Lord with all your heart and lean not on your own understanding."* Real leadership means loosening your grip and trusting God with the outcomes.

## Letting Go Is How Influence Grows

Letting go isn't passivity; it's trusting God more than your own grip. It makes room for others to grow, stumble, and rise. Legacy isn't built by clutching the spotlight but by sharing.

I grew up in a neighborhood church on Long Island, New York, where the motto was painted on the wall: *"Let go, let God."* As a boy, it sounded simple. Just let go, and God will handle it. But as I grew older, becoming a man, a husband, a father, and eventually a pastor, I discovered how hard those words are to live out.

I could not control circumstances. I could not control the choices my children made or the decisions of the people I pastored. Again and again, life reminded me that control was an illusion.

Only then did I understand what my childhood church was trying to teach: letting go is not a cliché, but a discipline. It is trusting God more than your own understanding (Proverbs 3:5).

Letting go creates space for others to lead, fail, grow, and rise. It is caring more about what God is doing than how people perceive you. It is handing off the mic, releasing outcomes, and celebrating others even when they do it differently. The moment you let go of control, influence begins to multiply.

When you lead from influence, not control, everything shifts. Your team grows more confident, your home more peaceful, and you rest easier, no longer carrying what God never assigned.

People may forget your strategy, but they will never forget your spirit. And when your spirit is **centered in Christ**, it does more than inspire; it unlocks others.

## Helping Others Step Into Their Futures

Unleashed leadership, in the end, isn't about the grandeur of your platform or the size of your audience. It's about authenticity; the raw, vulnerable, Spirit-filled journey that others watch and whisper, *"If they can rise, maybe I can too."*

When you break free, you light the way for others to follow. They don't just hear leadership; they catch it; like a spark igniting dry kindling, your passion becomes flame in those around you. That's the mystery of true influence: fire doesn't stay contained. It leaps, spreads, and warms everyone who draws near.

And that's when the real work begins: not just leading people, but unleashing them into who they were born to become. Because when you lead from overflow, not fear or fatigue, you don't simply manage outcomes; you multiply freedom. You fan embers into flame, and in your light others discover their own fire.

## Leaders Call Others to Rise

Sermons fade. Systems change. Strategies evolve. Positions change. But people, when empowered, carry your impact further than you ever could alone.

> **The truest legacy of a leader isn't what they build; it's who they unleash.**

You can preach with passion, lead with skill, and manage with excellence. But if those around you aren't rising with greater clarity, confidence, and conviction, your leadership hasn't multiplied. It's merely maintained.

Unleashed leaders think differently. They don't build platforms, they build people. They don't lead for applause, they lead for awakening. They see those they serve not as volunteers, staff, or followers, but as futures waiting to be unleashed.

This was Jesus's model. He didn't choose polished resumes. He chose fishermen, zealots, and tax collectors. He saw them not by their weaknesses or failures but through the lens of divine possibility. He called them forward, gave them access, and entrusted them with responsibility. That's what unleashed leaders do. They speak to who others are becoming, not just who they've been.

And you can do the same not just on a platform, but in hallway conversations, team huddles, car rides, and family dinners. Leadership isn't about supplying every answer, but guiding others to hear God's voice themselves.

Because the true power of unleashed leadership isn't just in what you teach; it's in who you activate.

## Leadership Is Multiplication, Not Just Management

One of the most evident signs of a healthy, unleashed leader is this: their presence doesn't shrink others; it *stretches* them. They don't dominate the room; they *develop* the room. They don't hoard knowledge; they *hand it off*. They don't micromanage; they *mentor*.

When others succeed, they don't feel threatened; they *celebrate*, then call them *higher*.

That's exactly what Paul did with Timothy. He didn't just pass along theology; he passed along a *legacy*; leadership grounded in conviction, endurance, and the heart to invest in others.

> *"And the things you have heard me say...entrust to reliable people who will also be qualified to teach others."*
> (2 Timothy 2:2)

And here's the invitation: you don't need a title to lead this way. You just need a willing heart and a vision big enough to include others.

Because unleashed leadership doesn't end with you; it *expands* through you.

Leadership belongs to anyone who sees people as carriers of the future. Maybe you're a youth pastor investing in a teenager, a parent shaping a child's character, or a leader who simply chooses to speak life into someone overlooked. Wherever you are, someone is watching how you lead, how you love, how you live.

Your unleashed life doesn't just transform *you*; it unlocks *them*.

If your breakthrough ends with you, so does your impact, but when what God does in you begins to multiply through you, a legacy is born. That's the result of unleashed leadership, not building monuments to your greatness, but movements that outlast your name.

## Succession: Reproducing What's Been Released in You

At some point, every leader must let go. Moses handed the baton to Joshua. Jesus empowered His disciples to carry the Gospel further. Paul charged Timothy to entrust what he'd received to others. In every case, the leader didn't just leave a position; they left a people equipped to keep building.

I once worked with an international and acclaimed leader who modeled this beautifully. After decades of building a thriving global organization, he didn't cling to power or position. With humility and clarity, he gathered his leaders, laid out the vision, and entrusted the baton to his successor. He understood that leadership isn't about how long you hold power but about ensuring the mission carries on after you.

Succession isn't about stepping aside; it's about stepping into the call of multiplication. Done with clarity and courage, it becomes a Spirit-led journey of legacy, release, and generational impact. When what God has done in you multiplies through others, your impact ripples for generations.

Your scars become someone else's survival guide. Your wisdom becomes their acceleration. Your ceiling becomes their floor. This is legacy leadership, not rooted in ego, but in eternity. And it begins with the courage to let go.

Every unleashed leader eventually reaches a pivotal moment when they realize: This is bigger than me. Embrace that moment. It's not shrinking your influence; it's expanding it. This is the handoff, the quiet shift from center stage to backstage, from holding on to lifting up, from being the one doing the work to becoming the one who builds others.

I've walked with leaders through these handoffs. Whether transitioning a church, developing a pipeline, or empowering emerging leaders, the process is emotional, complex, and deeply holy. But when it's led in alignment with the Spirit, it doesn't bind; it unlocks freedom, not only for you but for those who come after you.

You've started to unleash your leadership. Now the real question is: What would it look like to live completely unleashed?

CHAPTER 7

# Living Unleashed - Committing to Your Future

*Let us throw off everything that hinders...and run with perseverance the race marked out for us.*
— Hebrews 12:1 (NIV)

*"Your life does not get better by chance, it gets better by change."*[1]
— Jim Rohn

## The Power to Choose a New Future

By the age of forty-six, Jacqueline Kennedy Onassis had already buried two husbands and lost two children. Her grief made headlines, and the world wondered what was left for her. Yet behind the dark sunglasses and elegant smile was a woman who refused to let her story end in sorrow.

Instead of disappearing into the shadows of loss, she chose to begin again. She revisited a lifelong passion for writing and stepped into the world of publishing, not as a First Lady, but as an editor. Her surroundings no longer included kings and presidents but stacks of manuscripts waiting to be shaped. With the same determination that once reinvigorated the White House, she built a new chapter of her life.

"I have always lived through men," she confessed. "Now, I realize I can't do that anymore."[2]

And so, she didn't. Jackie didn't need a stage to reclaim her voice. She chose meaning over memory, future over fame. And in that quiet decision, she left us a blueprint: the future you long for won't be handed to you; you must choose it.

**Your Future and The Choice Beneath It All**

As a reminder, every day, you're moving toward one of four futures:

- **The Probable Future** — life on autopilot, where comfort and routine quietly call the shots.
- **The Plausible Future** — the safe zone, where you manage but rarely multiply.
- **The Possible Future** — the stretch of curiosity and hope, where you reach for what could be.
- **The Preferred Future** — the one God designed for you, rooted in calling, shaped by courage, and aligned with who He says you are.

Only one of these was created with you in mind. And at some point, you must decide: will you settle for what's easy, or commit to what God has prepared?

The Preferred Future isn't simple; it demands sacrifice. That's why the temptation to settle is so strong. For some, it shows up as preserving comfort; for others, avoiding the past or protecting against the pain of failure. Many drift endlessly in the probable, some flirt with possibility but never commit, and others stay stuck in the plausible, carefully managing what they already have but never multiplying influence, opportunities, or impact.

## You've Come Too Far to Play Small

You might not feel bold right now. You may still feel tender from a chapter that caught you off guard. You may look at your scars and wonder if you have what it takes.

But know this: you've already done hard things. You've already made courageous choices. You've already risen after the fall. You've already proven that fear doesn't get the final word.

And if no one's told you lately, hear it now, "You've come too far to play small!"

After you've battled through a hard season, there's often a quiet pull to retreat. Rarely does it shout. Normally, it's as small as a whisper. A new opportunity arises, but you question your readiness. A fresh idea stirs, but you talk yourself out of it before it can go anywhere. A relationship begins to heal, but you're afraid to trust it again.

And beneath it all, the question lingers: *"What if I try again…and it doesn't work?"*

But here's what I've learned and what Scripture reveals over and over: God doesn't bring you through transformation just for you to settle.

Israel had witnessed miracles firsthand and seen an awesome display of God's glory. Yet the moment things grew difficult, they cried out, 'Let's go back to Egypt' (Numbers 14:4)—not because Egypt was better, but because it was familiar.

## The Enemy Is Familiar, Not Failure

Familiarity whispers, *"Stay where it's safe. Don't risk the unknown."* But settling for what's familiar will always shrink your God-given future. You weren't born for smallness; you were born for kingdom impact, for leadership that awakens souls and leaves a legacy beyond your lifetime.

> **The enemy of your unleashed future isn't failure; it's familiarity.**

A pastor I coached once told me, *"I thought destiny meant launching campuses or preaching to thousands. But for me, it's been about standing tall in who I am, believing I don't have to apologize for the weight of my calling".*

Sometimes, standing is the boldest thing you can do. I'm reminded of a pivotal moment in Exodus, when Moses and the Israelites followed God out of Egypt, only to find themselves trapped between the Red Sea in front and Pharaoh's chariots behind.

## When Standing Is Enough

Imagine the heavy weight of leadership Moses felt. Perhaps he was even tempted to doubt everything God had spoken in that moment. But what does he tell them? "Stand still, and see the salvation of the Lord…" (Exodus 14:13). And we all know what happened after that.

That's what living unleashed is all about. You don't have to leap today, but you do need to stand. Stand in your calling. Stand in your clarity. Stand in your God-given identity. Because when you stand, you send a message to your family, to your team, to your church, and even to your own soul: *We are not playing small anymore.*

And once you've taken that stand, the next question is simple but vital: What now? How do you carry that resolve instead of letting it fade?

## Ready for What Comes Next

Living unleashed doesn't mean being reckless; it means being ready. It doesn't mean jumping at everything. It doesn't mean saying yes to burnout, chaos, or every opportunity that comes your way. Unleashed means you're released from hesitation and no longer lead from fear.

You are no longer waiting for perfect conditions. You're no longer trapped in comparison or paralyzed by imposter syndrome. You're no longer letting shame have a vote in your decisions.

Instead, you're grounded: in who you are, in what matters most, and where God is pointing you next.

That's what living unleashed looks like: Not perfection, not arrogance, but a steady, grounded willingness to move forward with God; even when the ground feels shaky.

## Living Unleashed Isn't Someday; It's Right Now

Your legacy doesn't start later; it's being built today. Every decision, every conversation, every quiet "yes" to God is shaping the future of your family, your church, your team, and your community right now.

Living unleashed doesn't wait for a stage. It shows up in the sphere you already have: mentoring someone who's watching, modeling grace when conflict rises, staying true when compromise whispers.

You don't need a platform to leave a mark. You need a posture of availability, alignment, and obedience. But the moment you rise with that posture, another voice always rises too.

## An Old Familiar Voice

It slithers like a snake, silently whispers in your ear:

*"Be careful."*
*"Don't reach too far."*
*"Play it safe this time."*
*"Don't you remember what happened last time?"*

It disguises itself as wisdom. It masquerades as maturity. It whispers that boldness is reckless and risk is irresponsible.

Here's what I've learned: boldness doesn't always feel like fire; it often feels like a trembling voice. Sometimes it looks like simply showing up again when it would be easier to stay home.

And let's be clear: boldness isn't recklessness; it's a response to clarity. When God begins to stir something new, whether a dream, a shift, a healing, or a release, the urge to protect yourself will feel noble.

That facade of wisdom is, in reality, the echo of past pain trying to get you to "play it safe." But safety isn't the same as peace, and that's where many of us get stuck.

## Unleashing Boldness Over Safety

Many believers confuse safety with peace. They assume that if something stretches them, it must not be from God. If it disrupts their current rhythm, costs them comfort, or forces them to face insecurity, it must be a sign to stop.

Read your Bible. Rarely, if ever, does God call someone to a small, manageable assignment.

He calls Abram to leave everything he's known.
He calls Moses to confront Pharaoh.
He calls Esther to risk her life.
He calls Peter out of the boat.
He calls Paul into persecution.
He calls Mary to carry a scandalous miracle.
He calls Jesus to bear a cross.

God's Will is rarely comfortable, but it is always consecrated. You can be sure it will be set apart, purposeful, and worth it. If boldness feels costly, you're likely right where you're supposed to be.

So why do so many of us hesitate? Why, after walking through healing, growth, and revelation, do we still feel the urge to shrink back? More often than not, it's not because we lack vision; it's because we're battling fear. Here are three of the most common fears that keep leaders playing small:

## The Three Fears That Keep Leaders Playing Small

1. **Fear of Being Misunderstood**
   You've seen what happens when you speak up. You've lived through misalignment and painful conversations. You don't want to rock the boat. So, you water it down. You settle. You play nice. But unleashed leaders don't thrive by being liked. They lead with clarity, integrity, and love, and they trust that time will reveal their heart.

2. **Fear of Failure**
   You've tried before. Maybe you launched something that didn't grow. Maybe you led people who walked away. Maybe you dreamed too loudly, and reality came crashing in. But failure isn't the opposite of progress; it's the path to it. Nobody builds anything meaningful without risk. And every time you choose bold obedience, even if it doesn't "succeed" the way you expected, you grow stronger.

3. **Fear of Being Too Much**
   This one runs especially deep for women in ministry and the marketplace. You've been told to tone it down. You've been accused of being intimidating, too emotional, too spiritual, too serious…so you learn to shrink. But unleashed living means you refuse to apologize for your assignment. You don't dominate, but you also don't disappear. You step fully into your space, graced, grounded, and unafraid to shine.

## Boldness Is Contagious

When you choose to live unleashed, the ripple effect begins. Your kids start to see what faith looks like in motion. Your staff starts dreaming again. Your marriage regains its spark. Your ministry catches wind. Your team starts asking better questions. Your church shifts from maintenance to mission.

Why? Because courage is contagious. Boldness, especially when modeled in humility, gives everyone else permission to rise. It awakens hope, stirs vision, and creates movement.

This is the kind of power that doesn't stop with you but spills over into every space you touch. It reshapes your home, your church, your community, and the legacy you leave behind.

But it doesn't happen by chance.

## You Don't Drift into Destiny—You Decide Into It

We love the idea that one day, we'll "get there." That if we keep doing what we're doing, eventually the right doors will open, the perfect alignment will happen, and everything we've dreamed will fall into place. But the future doesn't happen by accident. It's built through alignment and sustained through commitment.

You can prepare, journal, brainstorm, and strategize, but at some point, to live unleashed, you will have to decide. You have to commit to the future you say you want. Beyond theory and wishful thinking, your actions must align with the future you desire. It must be pursued with all the faith, focus, and intentionality you can muster, because **the life you want is not built by your intentions but by the direction of your decisions.**

There's a reason so many pivotal moments in Scripture begin with a choice:

*Choose this day whom you will serve…"* (Joshua 24:15)
*"Here I am. Send me."* (Isaiah 6:8)
*"If anyone wants to be My disciple, they must…"* (Luke 9:23)

God doesn't bulldoze His way into our destiny. He invites us to step into it with Him. And while we don't control the outcome, we *do* control the offer. We get to bring our time, our attention, our energy, and our obedience, and lay it before Him as worship.

But before you can commit to building the future God has for you, you have to get honest about something simple and yet much harder to pin down:

## What Do You Actually Want?

Before we talk about commitment, I need to ask you something: What do you actually want? And I need you to give the honest answer, not the Instagram version or the version that will impress your pastor, your board, your neighbors, or peers. We aren't talking about the version someone else scripted for you, but your *preferred* future, the leader God says you are. Ask yourself:

- What kind of leader do I want to become?
- What kind of culture do I want to create?
- What kind of legacy do I want to leave?
- What kind of faith do I want to walk in?
- What kind of person do I want to be when no one is watching?

God is nudging something in you, and once you're clear on what you want, you can align your life around it, not in anxiety or hustle, but in holy commitment.

Clarity is a gift. But clarity without commitment still leaves you stuck. At some point, you have to build what God has revealed.

## Commitment Leaves a Trail

If your future had a camera, what would it see you doing today? Commitment always shows up somewhere: how you spend your time, where you give your energy, the words you speak over yourself, and the way you rise after setbacks. The future isn't built by dramatic declarations but by daily devotion. Quiet faithfulness. Obedient steps. Consistent surrender.

And when progress feels slow, it's easy to believe you've fallen too far behind, that you've missed your moment. But no matter how far you feel from the life you want, you're just one decision away from building again.

## What You Commit To, You Become

You might not feel bold today. That's okay. You might still be shaking off disappointment. That's okay. But if you want a different outcome, you need a different commitment, not out of guilt or pressure, but out of conviction.

You're the only one who can say yes to the life God is calling you toward. You don't need every detail worked out; you just need to be all-in with the part He's placed in your hands. And when you are, it's more than enough for God to move through, shaping your future as only He can.

## Unleashed Doesn't Mean Perfect—It Means Free

It means leading with authenticity, not armor. It means moving forward even when you still feel the quake in your knees. It means you've decided fear and failure won't be your guides anymore.

It means you've stopped letting your past determine your pace. It means you're no longer apologizing for your voice, your calling, your values, or your anointing. It means you're not bound anymore.

I know a man who has spoken at thousands of engagements, on six continents, to hundreds of thousands, if not millions of people. And even as he speaks, his knees still quiver, and his hands still tremble as if it were the first time he were preaching. But he does it anyway, because his freedom is not contained by his imperfection.

## Perfection Is a Prison—And You Were Meant to Live Free

God never asked you to be perfect; He asked you to be present. Yet, so many of us grow up believing that to be effective we must be impressive; to be impactful we must be polished; to be powerful we must hide our brokenness.

> **Perfection is a prison, and you were never meant to live locked inside it**

Ironically, when you stop trying to be impressive, you become influential. People don't follow perfect; they follow real, consistent, and free.

## Grace Is the Fuel for a Sustainable Future

Presence alone isn't enough; you need grace to carry you. Without it, you'll grind harder, say yes to too much, and shoulder burdens God never asked you to hold. Grace reminds you: You don't carry this alone. You're not the savior of your family, church, or community. You're not the solution to every problem.

Grace breaks chains of performance, loosens the grip of shame, and breathes fresh vision into weary places. *Grace is the fuel* that frees you to live unleashed.

## The Real You Is the Free You

Somewhere inside, the real you is still there: the version who dreams without fear. Who speaks up without second-guessing. Who doesn't shrink to fit others' comfort. Who remembers what joy feels like.

That version isn't an illusion; it's your spirit before it got buried under expectations and exhaustion. And guess what? That version is coming back. One decision at a time. One brave yes after another. One whispered prayer when no one sees you.

The world doesn't need a more polished version of you; it needs the free version. The bold one. The kind one. The curious one. The rooted one. The one God created and is calling out again.

And when that version rises, it's not just your future that changes; it's the people around you, the legacy you leave, and the Kingdom impact you make.

## So Let This Be the Season You Stop Holding Back

You've done the work. You've wrestled the hard truths. You've confronted the past. You've realigned your values. You've rebuilt with small bricks. You've walked through unforeseen challenges and come out wiser.

Now is the time to rise. Not in a rush, but in rhythm. Not in pride, but in peace. Not in hype, but in holy fire.

You were never meant to live contained. You were meant to live unleashed. And now, everything in you is being invited to rise, to step beyond surviving and start fully living.

This is more than the end of a chapter. It's the turning of a page in your own life.

The you who started this journey is not the same you standing here now. You've faced hard truths. You've stared down old mindsets. You've felt the tremors of uncertainty and stood anyway. You've started building again, with grace, with clarity, and with a brick-by-brick faith.

Now comes the invitation not just to *dream* about your future…but to *live into it*. Not with pressure, but with purpose. Not by striving, but by aligning.

Your future is not fixed.
It's unfolding.
And it's waiting for you to rise—**unleashed**.

## CONCLUSION

# Living Unleashed: Your Future Is a Decision Away

*See, I am doing a new thing! Now it springs up; do you not perceive it?*
— Isaiah 43:19 (NIV)

*"You can't go back and change the beginning, but you can start where you are and change the ending."*[1]
— attributed to C.S. Lewis

### The Edge of the Unleashed Life

You made it to the close of this book, and the opening of *your* next great chapter!

You've journeyed through the landscapes of the four futures: probable, plausible, possible, and preferred. You've walked through divine disruptions and detours and learned to see them not as delays but holy altars.

You've forged new mindsets in the fire, broken agreements with fear, reclaimed the God-given power to choose, rediscovered purpose beneath the rubble, and with trembling hands, picked up your brick to build again.

You've done more than read. You've remembered who you are.

But before you step into what's next, pause with me for one final moment. There's one more truth I need you to understand:

Your future isn't waiting for perfect timing; it's waiting for your "yes". A "yes" that chooses, right here and right now, what tomorrow will be.

Because the future isn't discovered. It's constructed. And construction begins with a decision.

## The Call: Not to Do More, But to Live Aligned

This journey was never about more hustle. It was about discovering a deeper harmony.

When your values speak in harmony with your voice, when your daily rhythm flows with your deepest vision, when your presence reflects the purpose God planted inside you…you can do more than live well. You can live and lead *unleashed*.

## Your Destiny Is Built by Three Sacred Tools

By now, you've seen it: prayer anchors, purpose fuels, and choice moves you into action. Together, they unleash divine momentum—the blueprint of destiny.

And now, the invitation is yours.

## Your Commissioning Moment

If I could sit across from you right now, I'd tell you this: You don't need permission to lead boldly. You don't need to shrink so others can rise. You don't have to carry every burden alone. You are not too late; you are right on time.

Say "yes". "Yes" to God's whisper of courage. "Yes" to building when no one claps. "Yes" to living with vision and leading with fire. "Yes" to becoming the person your future needs you to be.

Because your yes today is more than a decision; it's a ripple that sets others free.

The journey doesn't end here. It begins here.

**Unleash 40-Day Future Shift Devotional** *Not perfection. Not performance. Just 40 days of faithfulness that shape your future.*

That's what the *Unleash* 40-Day Future Shift Devotional invites you into, not a sprint, but a steady, Spirit-led rhythm. This is your moment to turn every insight, every shift, every whisper from God into consistent, courageous action.

Each day: a small shift in mindset.
Each step: a deeper alignment between who you are and who you're becoming.
Each week: momentum, not from striving harder, but from showing up faithfully.

One prayer. One surrender. One act of courage. One Kingdom habit. The future is built not by performance, but by faithful partnership with God.

# A Final Prayer

Father,

Thank You for the one reading these words.
For their heart to grow, to lead, to heal, and to build.
Fill them with boldness, and strengthen them when fear whispers.
Let their life reflect Your glory and overflow with Your grace.

Make joy their rhythm, grace their covering, and courage their song.
Align their steps, not driven by fear, but drawn by love.
And let this next chapter be marked by joy, purpose, and divine momentum.

In Jesus' name, Amen.

## A Personal Word from Dr. Brawley

If no one has told you lately, let me be the first to say: I believe in you. Not because you are perfect, but because you have purpose. I believe in the purpose of God in your life and know that when ordinary people say yes to God in extraordinary ways, history shifts.

So go build. Live with vision. Lead with fire. Live unleashed—and never look back.

**Appendix: Tools to Help You Build the Future You Were Born For**

I want to leave you with practical tools you can use right now. These aren't just ideas — they're frameworks you can put into practice today. Inside this appendix, you'll find:

- **The Four Futures Framework (Summary Chart)** – A quick reference to help you identify whether you're heading toward a probable, possible, plausible, or preferred future.
- **The 1% Rule Worksheet** – A simple exercise to help you turn small, consistent actions into sacred steps of transformation.
- **Reflection Questions** – Prompts that will help you slow down, listen to God, and apply what you've read in your own context.

These are designed to get you started. But there's more waiting for you…

*Want the full set of tools — including expanded worksheets, bonus exercises, and updated resources?*

Download the **Unleash Digital Toolkit** at **donbrawley.com/unleash.**

When you sign up, you'll also receive:

- Exclusive updates and leadership insights from me.
- Bonus resources I couldn't fit in this book.
- Early access to future trainings, masterclasses, and events.

*Think of it as your next step in living unleashed.*

Want the expanded Team Worksheet — including writing space, reflection prompts, and a facilitator's guide? Download it free at donbrawley.com/Unleash.

## APPENDIX A

# Four Futures Discernment Tool

| Possible Future | Preferred Future |
|---|---|
| Signs:<br>• You start to dream again and envision what life could look like.<br>• Creativity, passion, and courage begin to stir.<br>• Hope rises, but momentum feels fragile without prayer, planning, and action.<br><br>Personal Check: Am I willing to act on the God-sized possibilities stirring in my heart? | Signs:<br>• You have clarity about what matters most and live by it daily.<br>• Prayer and faith fuel decisions, not just convenience.<br>• Life shows alignment between who you are, what you do, and what God is calling you to.<br><br>Personal Check: Am I building my life with both faith and intentionality surrendering what I want for what God wants for me? |

| Plausible Future | Probable Future |
|---|---|
| The "safe" or manageable future—what feels reasonable but keeps you limited.<br><br>Signs:<br>• You rely on routines that are comfortable but uninspiring.<br>• You set goals that feel cautious rather than courageous.<br>• Growth feels slow because fear of risk outweighs bold obedience.<br><br>Personal Check: Am I settling for what feels safe rather than stepping into what God is truly calling me to? | The trajectory you're on if nothing changes.<br><br>Signs:<br>• Daily life feels more about maintenance than momentum.<br>• Energy and passion begin drifting downward.<br>• You sense yourself repeating cycles instead of moving forward.<br><br>Personal Check: Am I passively drifting into a future I never would have chosen? |

Want the expanded Individual or Team Worksheet, including writing space, reflection prompts, and additional resources? Download it free at donbrawley.com/unleash.

## APPENDIX B

# Four Futures Discernment Tool for Church Leadership Teams

| Possible Future | Preferred Future |
|---|---|
| The stretch of curiosity and hope, what could be if faith and imagination take root. | The God-designed future—aligned with your mission, calling, vision, and intentional leadership. |
| Signs: Leaders dream out loud and envision new impact. Spirit-led creativity begins to stir. Momentum is fragile, needs prayer and planning to take root. | Signs: Mission and values clearly shape decisions. Alignment exists between prayer, vision, and action. Culture of multiplication, renewal, and Spirit-empowered growth. |
| Leadership Check: Are we willing to act on the God-sized possibilities stirring in our hearts? | Leadership Check: Are we building with both faith and intentionality toward the future God has called us to fulfill? |

| Plausible Future | Probable Future |
|---|---|
| The "safe" or manageable future, what seems reasonable but keeps the church stagnant. | The default future—the trajectory you're on if nothing changes. |
| Signs: Dependable routines, but little innovation or risk. Goals feel cautious rather than compelling. Comfort outweighs faith-filled action. | Signs: Meetings focused mostly on maintenance. Energy and engagement drifting downward. Ministry impact diminishes slowly but steadily. |
| Leadership Check: Are we managing well but failing to step into what God is calling us toward? | Leadership Check: Are we passively drifting into a future we never would have chosen? |

## Team Exercise:

1. Ask leaders to place the church in the quadrant they feel represents today.
2. Compare perceptions and discuss gaps.
3. Ask: *What deliberate choices would move us toward the Preferred Future?*

## APPENDIX C

# The 1% Rule for Your Preferred Future

**The 1% Rule**

Transformation doesn't come through giant leaps — it comes through small, consistent steps that compound over time. What's one 1% shift you can make today to move closer to the future God has designed for you?

**Steps:**

1. Identify one area where you sense God calling you to grow.
2. Name one small, consistent action that would move you forward.
3. Anchor it with a Scripture or biblical truth.
4. Share it with someone for accountability.
5. After 30 days, reflect on the fruit and adjust as needed.

Want the expanded Team Worksheet — including writing space, reflection prompts, and a facilitator's guide? Download it free at donbrawley.com/unleash.

## APPENDIX D

# The 1% Rule for Team's Preferred Future

### The 1% Rule for Teams

Culture doesn't change overnight. It shifts one small step at a time. The 1% Rule helps leadership teams make small, consistent changes that add up to lasting transformation.

**Steps for Your Team:**

1. **Name Your Preferred Future** – Where is God calling your team to grow?
2. **Choose a 1% Shift** – Identify one small, consistent action you will practice together.
3. **Anchor It in Scripture** – Choose a verse or truth that will remind you why this matters.
4. **Set a Rhythm** – Decide when and how often you'll practice it (daily, weekly, every meeting).
5. **Build Accountability** – Assign someone to track progress and celebrate stories.

6. **Reflect and Adjust** – After 30 days, ask: what fruit do we see? What's our next 1% shift?

Want the expanded Team Worksheet — including writing space, reflection prompts, and a facilitator's guide? Download it free at donbrawley.com/unleash.

## APPENDIX E

# Chapter Reflection Questions

**Chapter 1: Four Futures—Discerning the One You Were Born For**
1. Which of the four futures (probable, possible, plausible, preferred) best describes where you're currently headed — and why?
2. Where do you see signs of drifting versus intentional building in your life or leadership?
3. What does your *preferred future* look like when you imagine it in light of God's calling on your life?

**Chapter 2: The Blueprint—Building God's Future in Your Life**
1. What small, consistent actions have shaped your present reality — for better or for worse?
2. Where do you sense God calling you to begin "laying bricks" differently?
3. If someone watched your daily choices for the next 30 days, what kind of future would they see you building?

## Chapter 3: The Fire Your Future Depends On
1. What limiting belief, past failure or old story do you need to release in order to step into God's future for you?
2. Where have you been settling for the *probable* future when God is calling you to the *preferred* one?
3. What spiritual practice or truth could help you rewrite the story you tell yourself?

## Chapter 4: Unleashed Power—The Quiet Yes That Sparks Revival
1. Where in your life do you need to tap into God's power instead of relying solely on your own strength?
2. How would your leadership shift if you operated more from overflow than from overwhelm?
3. Who in your circle needs you to model Spirit-led courage right now?

## Chapter 5: Break Free for a New Future
1. Where have you been clinging to control instead of exercising godly influence?
2. What is one area of your leadership where you need to surrender outcomes to God?
3. How might shifting from control to influence free others to step into their own calling?

## Chapter 6: Unleash the Leader Within
1. In what ways is your leadership currently shaping the future of others — intentionally or unintentionally?
2. What practices help you lead from a place of vision, fire, and overflow?
3. Who is one emerging leader you can invest in to multiply Kingdom impact?

**Conclusion: Living Unleashed—Committing to Your Future**
1. What "yes" do you need to give God today in order to step toward your preferred future?
2. How will you keep your altar (your place of surrender and dependence on God) alive as you move forward?
3. What bold first step can you take this week to live unleashed?

# Endnotes

**Introduction: When the Future You're Living No Longer Fits the One You Were Born For**
1. John Sculley, attributed: "The future belongs to those who see possibilities before they become obvious." Widely cited in secondary sources; a definitive first publication has not been located.
2. Winston Churchill, attributed: "Success is not final, failure is not fatal: it is the courage to continue that counts." No verified source in Churchill's writings or speeches; included here as a commonly attributed quotation.

**Chapter 1: Four Futures – Discerning the One You Were Born to Build**
1. Henry Blackaby and Claude King, *Experiencing God* (Nashville: B&H Publishing, 1990), xx.
2. Richard A. Slaughter, *Futures Beyond Dystopia: Creating Social Foresight* (London: Routledge, 2004).
3. Carol S. Dweck, *Mindset: The New Psychology of Success* (New York: Ballantine, 2006), 7.

**Chapter 2: The Blueprint – Building God's Future in Your Life**
1. Peter F. Drucker (attributed); this phrase appears commonly but has not been located in his published works.

2. James Clear, *Atomic Habits: An Easy & Proven Way to Build Good Habits and Break Bad Ones* (New York: Avery, 2018), 15.

## Chapter 3: The Fire Your Future Depends On
1. Attributed, source unknown: "The Holy Spirit can only fill a vessel that is empty, and He is waiting to fill us with fire. The fire of God never falls on dry wood; He falls on hearts that are ready and willing to burn."

## Chapter 4: Unleashed Power — The Quiet Yes That Shakes Nations
1. Hudson Taylor, attributed: "When we work, we work. When we pray, God works."
2. The Billy Graham prayer at John Wesley's home is a commonly retold anecdote; an original primary source is not located. For a representative retelling, see Historymakers Radio, "Billy Graham [Godspot]."
3. The Navigators, *Topical Memory System* (Colorado Springs: NavPress, 1969).
4. Simon Sinek, *Start with Why: How Great Leaders Inspire Everyone to Take Action* (New York: Portfolio, 2009).
5. Attributed, source unknown: "You're born looking like your parents, but you die looking like your decisions."

## Chapter 5: Breaking Free for a New Future
1. John Ortberg, *The Me I Want to Be: Becoming God's Best Version of You* (Grand Rapids: Zondervan, 2009).
2. Daniel G. Amen, *Change Your Brain, Change Your Life* (New York: Times Books, 1998).
3. Jennifer Garvey Berger, *Unlocking Leadership Mindtraps: How to Thrive in Complexity* (Stanford, CA: Stanford University Press, 2019).

### Chapter 6: Unleash the Leader Within
1. Jack Welch, attributed: "Before you are a leader, success is all about growing yourself. When you become a leader, success is all about growing others." See Jack Welch Management Institute, "What 'Leadership' Means to JWMI Alumni," Dec 13, 2019. Jack Welch Management Institute
2. Nelson Mandela, *Long Walk to Freedom: The Autobiography of Nelson Mandela* (Boston: Little, Brown, 1994). For selected prison-era statements, see the Nelson Mandela Foundation, "Selected quotes."

### Chapter 7: Living Unleashed – Committing to the Future You Desire
1. Jim Rohn, attributed: "Your life does not get better by chance, it gets better by change."
2. Jacqueline Kennedy Onassis, attributed: "I have always lived through men… Now, I realize I can't do that anymore."

### Conclusion
1. C.S. Lewis (attributed); this quotation is widely circulated online but does not appear in his published works (commonly misattributed to Lewis).

# Meet Dr. Don Brawley III

Dr. Don Brawley III is a trusted voice to leaders navigating both the marketplace and ministry. With over 30 years as a pastor and 20 years as a coach to executives, entrepreneurs, and church leaders, a Doctor of Strategic Leadership from Regent University and advanced training in Artificial Intelligence from the University of Oxford's Saïd Business School, he has also served the vision of influential ministry leaders such as Bishop Dale C. Bronner, Dr. Samuel R. Chand, and Bishop Tudor Bismark.

As an executive coach, Dr. Brawley has worked with C-Suite leaders and mid-level managers at global companies including Uber, Salesforce, Microsoft, KPMG, Coca-Cola, and Northwestern Mutual. His coaching has helped leaders execute strategy, transform culture, and drive results—empowering them to step boldly into their next season of growth with clarity and conviction while building the future where their organizations thrive.

As a consultant to local churches, Dr. Brawley helps pastors and ministry teams engage in strategic planning, lead culture transformation, and achieve organizational alignment so their congregations can flourish. He has come alongside church leaders to unleash their God-given potential, align vision with calling, and cultivate ministry cultures where people thrive and Kingdom impact multiplies.

A pastor, consultant, and leadership coach, Dr. Brawley is also a leadership strategist and AI architect. As the founder of **Don Brawley Consulting**, he blends biblical insight with practical leadership tools, innovative strategy, and emerging technologies to ignite transformation and build futures marked by growth, influence, and lasting impact. He resides in Atlanta, Georgia, with his wife, Mona, of more than 37 years, and together they enjoy life and ministry with their three adult children and their families.

# Church and Marketplace Consulting Services

**Church Consulting Services**
- **Church Alignment** – Align vision, strategy, and structure to maximize Kingdom impact.
- **Team Shift** – Strengthen leadership teams to work with clarity, unity, and effectiveness.
- **Culture Creation** – Build healthy, Spirit-led cultures where people and ministries thrive.
- **Succession Planning** – Equip churches to transition leadership smoothly and faithfully.
- **Strategic Planning** – Create actionable plans that move your church toward its preferred future.

**Marketplace Consulting Services**
- **Organizational Alignment** – Align people, strategy, and structure to accelerate results.
- **Team Performance** – Strengthen teams to execute with clarity, collaboration, and impact.
- **Culture Transformation** – Shape healthy, high-performing cultures that sustain growth.
- **Leadership Transitions** – Equip leaders to step into new roles with confidence and continuity.

- **Strategic Planning** – Design actionable strategies that move your organization toward its preferred future.

www.donbrawley.com
www.futurereadychurch.ai

# The V.M.O.C. Framework™

*(Vision · Ministry · Operations · Culture)*

*Harnessing AI to strengthen **vision**, empower **ministry**, simplify **operations**, and protect **culture**.*

### 1. Vision — Aligning AI with the Preferred Future
- Help pastors and boards discern their **preferred future** and create a roadmap where AI becomes a servant, not a master.
- Use AI-driven insights (attendance, giving, community trends) to clarify vision and strategy.
- Train leaders to use AI as a **discernment partner** — giving better data so they can make Spirit-led decisions.

### 2. Ministry — Equipping Leaders to Shepherd with AI
- **Sermon research and study** tools that save time while keeping the pastor's authentic voice.
- **Discipleship personalization** — AI-guided pathways that help members grow in their walk with Christ.
- **Pastoral care systems** that track needs, prayer requests, and follow-ups so no one falls through the cracks.

### 3. Operations — Lightening the Load of Administration
- Automating repetitive tasks: scheduling, bulletins, volunteer coordination.

- Enhancing donor engagement and management through AI-powered CRM tools.
- Creating smart workflows so staff spend less time on paperwork and more time on people.

**4. Culture — Building Ethical & Spirit-Led Guardrails**
- Equip churches with **biblical principles for AI use** — ensuring technology supports rather than replaces Spirit-led leadership.
- Facilitate conversations about **ethics, transparency, and trust** so congregations feel safe.
- Create a culture where AI is seen as a **tool for Kingdom impact**, not a threat to faith.

Dr. Brawley offers:
- **One-time workshops** (introducing the V.M.O.C. Framework).
- **Consulting packages** (deep dive into one or all four areas).
- **Group coaching** cohorts for pastors and leadership teams designed to help church leaders integrate vision, culture, and strategy in community with others.

www.donbrawley.com
www.futurereadychurch.ai

www.ingramcontent.com/pod-product-compliance
Lightning Source LLC
Chambersburg PA
CBHW052052070526
44584CB00017B/2138